# Cocaine and Crack

by Tamara L. Roleff

**Drugs**

ReferencePoint Press™

San Diego, CA

**For more information, contact**
ReferencePoint Press, Inc.
PO Box 27779
San Diego, CA 92198
www.ReferencePointPress.com

Picture credits:
Maury Aaseng, 31–34, 48–51, 64–67, 81–84
AP/Wide World Photos, 17
Photos.com, 9

Series design:
Tamia Dowlatabadi

LIBRARY OF CONGRESS CATALOGING-IN-PUBLICATION DATA

Roleff, Tamara L., 1959–
    Cocaine and crack / by Tamara L. Roleff.
        p. cm. — (Compact research)
    Includes bibliographical references and index.
    ISBN-13: 978-1-60152-001-2 (hardback)
    ISBN-10: 1-60152-001-8 (hardback)
    1. Cocaine abuse—United States—Juvenile literature. 2. Crack (Drug)—United States—Juvenile literature. I. Title.
    HV5825.R647 2008
    362.29'80973—dc22
                                                                    2007020164

# Contents

# Foreword

“ **Where is the knowledge we have lost in information?** ”

—"The Rock," T.S. Eliot.

As modern civilization continues to evolve, its ability to create, store, distribute, and access information expands exponentially. The explosion of information from all media continues to increase at a phenomenal rate. By 2020 some experts predict the worldwide information base will double every 73 days. While access to diverse sources of information and perspectives is paramount to any democratic society, information alone cannot help people gain knowledge and understanding. Information must be organized and presented clearly and succinctly in order to be understood. The challenge in the digital age becomes not the creation of information, but how best to sort, organize, enhance, and present information.

ReferencePoint Press developed the *Compact Research* series with this challenge of the information age in mind. More than any other subject area today, researching current events can yield vast, diverse, and unqualified information that can be intimidating and overwhelming for even the most advanced and motivated researcher. The *Compact Research* series offers a compact, relevant, intelligent, and conveniently organized collection of information covering a variety of current and controversial topics ranging from illegal immigration to marijuana.

The series focuses on three types of information: objective single-author narratives, opinion-based primary source quotations, and facts and statistics. The clearly written objective narratives provide context and reliable background information. Primary source quotes are carefully selected and cited, exposing the reader to differing points of view. And facts and statistics sections aid the reader in evaluating perspectives. Presenting these key types of information creates a richer, more balanced learning experience.

For better understanding and convenience, the series enhances information by organizing it into narrower topics and adding design features that make it easy for a reader to identify desired content. For example, in *Compact Research: Illegal Immigration*, a chapter covering the economic impact of illegal immigration has an objective narrative explaining the various ways the economy is impacted, a balanced section of numerous primary source quotes on the topic, followed by facts and full-color illustrations to encourage evaluation of contrasting perspectives.

The ancient Roman philosopher Lucius Annaeus Seneca wrote, "It is quality rather than quantity that matters." More than just a collection of content, the *Compact Research* series is simply committed to creating, finding, organizing, and presenting the most relevant and appropriate amount of information on a current topic in a user-friendly style that invites, intrigues, and fosters understanding.

# Cocaine and Crack a Glance

## What Are Cocaine and Crack?

Cocaine, a stimulant, is one of the oldest drugs in use. Crack and cocaine are the same drug, just in different forms. Cocaine is a powder derived from the coca leaf that is sniffed or dissolved in water and injected. Crack is a more recent phenomenon, and is a derivative of cocaine.

## How Prevalent Is Cocaine/Crack Consumption?

The United States consumes 90 percent of Columbia's cocaine, or about 50 perecent of the world's cocaine produced, about 300 metric tons. The United States has the greatest rate of cocaine consumption among people aged 15–64, 2.8 percent.

## What Is the Scope of Cocaine Abuse in the United States?

In 2005 approximately 5.5 million Americans used cocaine during the past year. Approximately 33.5 million Americans older than age 12 (or 13.8 percent of the population) have tried cocaine at least once during their lifetime. Men abuse the drug more than women.

## What Are the Effects of Cocaine and Crack Use?

The short-term effects of cocaine use include euphoria, extra energy, and mental alertness. However, physiological symptoms include constricted blood vessels, dilated pupils, and increased temperature, heart rate, and blood pressure. Other effects include bizarre, erratic, and/or violent behavior, as well as tremors, vertigo, muscle twitches, and paranoia. Long-term effects include restlessness, irritability, anxiety, addiction, hallucinations, and mood disturbances. Long-term use can result in cardiac arrest, seizures, and death.

## How Does Cocaine Use Affect Fetal Development?

Cocaine can cross the placenta during pregnancy, but critics disagree about whether the mother's cocaine use causes long-term damage to the fetus. Babies whose mothers used crack or cocaine during pregnancy are often born premature or have low birth weights and are smaller than average.

## Does Cocaine Have a Legal Medical Use?

Cocaine was used until about 1916 as a tonic, patent medicine, and in beverages as a quick pick-me-up. Cocaine has been and continues to be used by doctors as a local anesthetic for some eye, nose, and throat surgeries. It also constricts blood vessels, which lessens bleeding during these surgeries.

## What Are the Laws Concerning Cocaine Use?

Possession of or trafficking in crack results in much harsher sentences than possession of or trafficking in powdered cocaine. Selling 50 grams of crack nets the same 10-year prison sentence as selling 5,000 grams of powder cocaine.

## The Sentencing Disparity Between Crack and Cocaine?

Despite nearly equal drug use rates among all racial groups in 2005, 82.3 percent of those convicted under federal crack laws were black, 8 percent were Hispanic, and 8.2 percent were white. Of those convicted for cocaine, 27.9 percent were black, 55.1 percent were Hispanic, and 15.4 percent were white.

## What Are the Treatment Options for Cocaine and Crack Addiction?

While no single treatment method is appropriate for all users, many addicts must go through a medical detoxification program in a controlled environment supervised by medical professionals. Counseling and behavioral therapy is a critical part of cocaine treatment plans. Relapses are common, even among those who have been clean for long periods.

# Overview

❝ The most addictive substance known to man? After crack appeared, the number of people using it or any other form of cocaine didn't skyrocket—it fell.❞

—Steve Chapman, "End Draconian Double-Standard on Cocaine Use."

❝ [Crack's] physical risks are bad enough, but its addictiveness takes crack way over the top, trouble-wise. Some experts call it the most addictive drug, and some users say they were addicted the moment they first put a pipe to their lips.❞

—Jim Parker, "Crack: Cocaine Squared."

Cocaine is the second most commonly used illicit drug (behind marijuana) in the United States. According to the 2005 National Survey on Drug Use and Health, 2.4 million Americans aged 12 and older used cocaine and 700,000 Americans used crack during the month prior to the survey. Cocaine is not legal in any country, but there is extensive debate over whether cocaine—and other illicit drugs—should be legalized.

## What Are Cocaine and Crack?

Cocaine is the most powerful natural stimulant drug known. It is derived from the coca leaf (*Erythroxylon coca*), which is grown in the Andes of South America. To transform coca leaves into cocaine, the leaves are mashed into a paste using sulfuric acid or kerosene, which is then allowed

*Cocaine, seen here in powder form, is the second most commonly used illicit drug (behind marijuana) in the United States.*

to dry into a powder. The result is cocaine hydrochloride, a salt-based form of the drug and highly soluble. Powdered cocaine is either inhaled (snorted) or dissolved in water and injected intravenously.

Cocaine can also be smoked, but the powdered hydrochloride cocaine must be changed into an alkaloid, or base (as opposed to salt) form of cocaine that can be smoked. Alkaloid cocaine is typically made by dissolving the powder in water, then adding a base such as ammonia (for freebase cocaine) or baking soda (for crack cocaine). The base cocaine precipitates in the solution, is filtered and dried, and then mixed with ether and smoked as freebase cocaine. Ether is extremely flammable, however, and many users, including comedian Richard Pryor, have been seriously burned while making or smoking freebase cocaine. Because of the dangers involved with freebase cocaine, many users prefer crack cocaine. The steps for filtering and adding ether are omitted when making crack. The "rocks" that are left are crack cocaine, which are chipped into smaller pieces and smoked in a crack pipe.

Cocaine does have a few legitimate medical applications, such as a local anesthesia for eye, nose, and throat surgeries. As such, it is a Schedule II drug, meaning it has a high risk of abuse.

## Slang Terms for Cocaine

Cocaine has many street names. Powdered cocaine is also known as coke, blow, snow, C, flake, toot, or nose candy. Crack, so called because of the crackling noise it makes when heated in a pipe, is also called rocks. Due to cocaine's high cost and the extreme pleasurable feelings users experienced, cocaine has also been described as the "champagne of drugs," "gold dust," "Cadillac of drugs," and the "caviar of recreational drugs."[1]

> " **Cocaine is the most powerful natural stimulant drug known.** "

## How Cocaine Is Used

Powdered cocaine can be snorted or injected; crack is smoked. To snort cocaine, a thin line of cocaine is inhaled into the nasal passages with a straw. Some users who inject cocaine heat the water solution prior to injection as it gives them an additional rush as the hot solution moves through their veins. To smoke cocaine, a crack rock is placed into a crack pipe or tube with a small piece of steel wool to act as a filter. The rock is heated with a lighter to vaporize the cocaine and then the fumes are inhaled.

The faster the drug gets into the user's bloodstream, the sooner the user feels the effects and the more intense the high is. Smoking and injecting cocaine produce the most immediate highs—usually within 3 to 5 seconds of administering the drug. Users who snort cocaine must normally wait three to five minutes for the cocaine to reach the bloodstream. However, the faster and more intense the high, the shorter the high lasts. The high from smoking or injecting cocaine lasts approximately 5 to 10 minutes, while the high from snorting lasts for about 15 to 30 minutes.

## How Cocaine Works

Dopamine is a chemical that transmits signals between nerve cells in the brain. During a rewarding experience, large amounts of dopamine are released, which makes the person feel good. In a normal brain, the dopamine binds with dopamine receptors, a special chemical that regulates the feelings of happiness. Cocaine disrupts the normal workings of the brain by blocking the dopamine receptors, causing a buildup of dopamine in the nerve cells, which in turn causes the feelings of euphoria associated with cocaine use.

However, the euphoria associated with cocaine is short-lived and is quickly followed by a crash. Following the high, the user will experience feelings of depression, irritability, anxiety, and fatigue. Many users will then take another dose of cocaine in an attempt to get back the high they had been enjoying just moments before. But the brain's ability to experience pleasure is limited. As more cocaine is ingested, the highs are never as high as they once were, leading the user to take a stronger and stronger dose of the drug in a futile attempt to reach the level of that first high.

## Historical Use

Native South Americans have been chewing the leaves of the coca plant or making a tea out of them for ceremonial and religious rituals for hundreds—if not thousands—of years. "Coca is an Andean tradition while cocaine is a Western habit,"[2] said former Bolivian president Paz Zamora in a 1992 speech before the World Health Organization. Cocaine became a Western habit at the end of the nineteenth and beginning of the twentieth centuries. In 1884 the young psychiatrist Sigmund Freud tried cocaine, proclaimed it "a magical drug,"[3] and urged his fiancée, friends, patients, and coworkers to try it. One colleague who tried the drug was Karl Koller, an intern in ophthalmology. He discovered one of the few legitimate uses for cocaine: as an anesthetic for eye surgery. As news spread about cocaine's euphoric properties, makers of patent remedies began including cocaine in their concoctions. Everything from cough syrups to wine—and a new soda drink called Coca-Cola—included a dose of cocaine, which was said to cure fatigue, depression, sleeplessness, morphine addiction, and even cancer.

> " Native South Americans have been chewing the leaves of the coca plant or making a tea out of them for ceremonial and religious rituals for hundreds—if not thousands—of years. "

## Health Effects

Cocaine was a very popular drug in the nineteenth century and it remains so today. One of the reasons why it became so popular was because it was believed that the drug was not addictive. Cocaine addicts do not show any of the typical physical symptoms of withdrawal, such as nausea and vomiting, abdominal pain, drenching sweats, nervousness and shaking, and seizures. Today, however, cocaine is known to be a very addictive drug. It is so addictive that "Mothers have given up their babies to get it,"[4] according to Alan I. Leshner, director of the National Institute on Drug Abuse (NIDA). Experiments have shown that lab mice addicted to cocaine will press a bar repeatedly to get a hit of cocaine, forsaking food, water, sleep, and sex, until they die.

> **Cocaine usage peaked during the 1980s and was the drug of choice among the affluent and powerful elite.**

Some of the short-term physical effects of using cocaine are increased energy, decreased appetite, mental alertness, increased heart rate and blood pressure, constricted blood vessels, and a fever. Long-term effects of cocaine use include drug tolerance resulting in more frequent and larger doses, addiction, irritability, restlessness, paranoia, and occasionally, hallucinations. Cocaine addiction can result in cardiac problems such as heart attacks and chaotic heart rhythms, chest pain and respiratory failure, strokes, seizures, headaches, and abdominal pain and nausea. Studies have also found that cocaine users are more likely to become infected with hepatitis C, have an increased risk of developing Parkinson's disease later in life, have a heart aneurysm, and dangerously high blood pressure.

## Restricting the Use of Cocaine

At the turn of the twentieth century, a public outcry about cocaine addiction led to changes in attitudes about cocaine use. The Harrison Narcotics Act was passed in 1914, ostensibly to regulate and tax doctors and pharmacists who prescribed and provided narcotic drugs (including cocaine). In actuality, though, it made providing drugs to addicts a crime, and many doctors were prosecuted and ruined professionally for prescribing drugs to their addicted patients. According to the editors of the *New York Medical Journal*, the results of the Harrison Narcotics Act were not a surprise. "As was expected . . . the immediate effects of the Harrison antinarcotic law were seen in the flocking of drug habitués to hospitals and sanatoriums. Sporadic crimes of violence were reported too, due usually to desperate efforts by addicts to obtain drugs, but occasionally to a delirious state induced by sudden withdrawal."[5]

Three years after the passage of the Harrison Narcotics Act, a committee appointed by the secretary of the treasury found that drug smuggling across U.S. borders with Canada and Mexico was a serious problem. The commission's recommendations to slow the increase in illegal drug use were strict enforcement of drug laws and the passage of more state laws similar to the Harrison Act.

## The Rise of Cocaine and Crack

Cocaine usage peaked during the 1980s and was the drug of choice among the affluent and powerful elite. Few people outside of celebrities, sports stars, and the wealthy could afford to indulge in cocaine; thus, cocaine addiction was not a serious problem in the United States simply because so few people could afford to buy the drug to get high.

However, crack put cocaine into the reach of addicts in even the lowest economic levels. While crack is a less pure form of cocaine (due to the addition of baking soda during the "cooking" process), smoking it provides a much more intense high than snorting powdered cocaine. Now a gram of powdered cocaine that formerly cost $100 or more per dose could be transformed into as many as 30 rocks of crack for as little as $5 to $10 each. Suddenly, anyone and everyone could afford crack cocaine. "What crack did was to lower dramatically the cost of the 'cocaine high,'" write John P. Morgan and Lynn Zimmer in *Crack in America: Demon Drugs and Social Justice*. "Simply because smoking delivers a drug more efficiently to the brain than does snorting, an amount of cocaine too small to produce an effect in powder form becomes an effective dose when converted to crack."[6]

> " **Crack put cocaine into the reach of addicts in even the lowest economic levels.** "

## Crack Fuels the Increase in Crime

Crack use eventually peaked in 1989. Early reports about crack co-caine claimed it was much more addictive, and therefore, much more dangerous than powdered cocaine. The claims of easy addiction were fueled by stories of crack addicts going on binges in crack houses. One reporter describes what crack addicts will go through to get high: "Addicts spend thousands of dollars on binges, smoking the contents of vial after vial in crack or 'base' houses—modern-day opium dens—for days at a time without food or sleep. They will do anything to repeat the high, including robbing their families and friends, selling their possessions and bodies."[7]

The dangers of crack extended to the community at large, as well. With the increasing popularity of crack came a skyrocketing gun-violence rate, especially among young black men of the nation's inner cities, who served as the cities' small-time crack dealers. The homicide rate among black teens 13 to 17 years old jumped nearly 500 percent as crack dealers fought to defend their turfs during crack's heyday.

## "Crack Babies"

A 1985 article in the *New England Journal of Medicine* suggested that crack could have a devastating effect on babies born to crack-addicted women. While the author suggested that more research be done on the issue, other newspapers and magazines picked up the story and soon there was a "crack baby" epidemic in the country. One social worker told *CBS News* that an 18-month-old baby she was caring for, who had been exposed to crack while still in the womb, would "barely be able to dress herself" because she would have "an IQ of perhaps 50."[8] Similar stories followed, filled with predictions of a "biological underclass" who were doomed to "a life of certain suffering, of probable deviance, of permanent inferiority."[9]

> "The fears of permanent damage in babies born to crack-addicted women appear to be unfounded.

However, the fears of permanent damage in babies born to crack-addicted women appear to be unfounded. Studies have found that poverty, malnutrition, cigarette smoking, and alcohol use during pregnancy have more of an effect on the health of a fetus than crack.

## Extent of Use in the United States

Although cocaine consumption is rapidly increasing in Europe, nearly two-thirds of cocaine users live in North and South America. North America claims almost half of the world's cocaine users, of which more than 40 percent live in the United States.

The 2005 National Survey on Drug Use and Health found that 33.7 million Americans aged 12 and older had tried cocaine at least once, while 5.5 million had used cocaine in the past year and 2.4 million had tried cocaine within the past month. The United Nations Office on Drugs and Crime found that the number of cocaine and crack users in the United States declined slightly between 2003 and 2004, from 2.5 percent of the population to 2.4 percent for cocaine; and from 0.6 percent to 0.5 percent

> " Nearly two-thirds of cocaine users live in North and South America. "

for crack. However, a better measurement of cocaine usage is the Monitoring the Future surveys, which track drug usage among 8th, 10th, and 12th graders. These surveys show that cocaine use declined from its peak in 1985 to its lowest point ever in 1992, then slowly started to rise again. In 1999, however, cocaine use among high school students started to fall again, and by 2005 usage had fallen by more than 20 percent. Overall, the percentage of high school students who used cocaine in 2005 is about 3.4 percent, about 60 percent lower than it was 20 years earlier during its peak.

## Sentencing Disparity

Public concern over the explosion in crack—and stories about its ability to instantly addict users after just one use—led Congress to pass the Anti-Drug Abuse Act of 1986. The law included the country's first mandatory minimum sentences; because crack was believed to be more dangerous than powder cocaine, crack possession was punished much more harshly than cocaine possession. Users convicted of possessing 5 grams of crack, which would provide no more than 50 doses, would receive a mandatory 5-year prison sentence. Defendants convicted of possessing powdered cocaine would have to have 500 grams of cocaine—100 times the minimum quantity for crack, and which breaks down to between 2,500 and 5,000 doses—in order to receive the same five-year sentence. Despite repeated attempts by opponents of the mandatory minimum sentences to change the 100-1 disparity rate between crack and cocaine, they have been unsuccessful.

## Treatment

The U.S. government spends billions of dollars trying to prevent cocaine use and treating those people who do abuse the drug. According to NIDA, "cocaine is the most commonly cited drug of abuse"[10] among treatment providers in most areas of the country. In addition, most people seeking treatment for cocaine addiction primarily smoke crack and often abuse more than one drug, which makes successful treatment more difficult.

Currently no drugs are available to mitigate the effects of cocaine addiction, as methadone is used for heroin. Therapists have determined that behavioral therapy—both in- and out-patient counseling—is "the only available, effective treatment approaches"[11] for treating cocaine addiction. But treating cocaine addiction is extremely difficult; users often suffer multiple relapses before kicking the habit for good. A relapse can be triggered by a sight, sound, smell, location, or being among people the addict associates with the drug.

> " The federal government works to decrease both the supply of cocaine overseas and the demand for cocaine at home. "

## The International War Against Cocaine

The war against cocaine is fought on many fronts and at many levels. The federal government works to decrease both the supply of cocaine overseas and the demand for cocaine at home. It provides financial aid, arms, training, and advisers to the South American governments of Colombia, Bolivia, and Peru to help eradicate the coca plant. Eradication efforts include aerial spraying of herbicides that kill the plants, as well as troops on the ground who find plots of coca bushes hidden in the jungles and pull them out by hand.

The U.S. government also provides the forces who intercept cocaine shipments as they are smuggled into the country. The Coast Guard, Border

*In March 2007 the U.S. DEA intercepted 19.4 metric tons of cocaine off the coast of Panama. The seized shipment was one of the biggest maritime busts anywhere on record.*

Patrol, National Guard, and Drug Enforcement Administration all work to interdict cocaine shipments. Despite five consecutive years of record-setting increases in cocaine interdiction, the United States is not experiencing a shortage of cocaine or a reduction in demand. In fact, the National Drug Intelligence Center, a federal agency that provides annual reports on drug trafficking and abuse, estimates that the 2005 cocaine production is up sharply due to the discovery of new coca fields in areas not previously known for growing the coca bushes.

## Domestic Drug Policies

In the United States, the drug war is fought by attempting to educate youth about the dangers of cocaine and to reduce demand for cocaine. But, as the NDIC reports in its 2007 *National Drug Threat Assessment*, demand for cocaine is stable, neither increasing nor decreasing since 2002.

While the federal government remains firm in its policy that all illicit drug use is a punishable crime, many cities and some states are beginning to relax their drug policies. Many drug offenders are being sent to drug courts, which allow users to complete a treatment program instead of being sent to prison, to help them overcome their addiction. Some maintain that the best way to regulate drug use is to legalize illicit drugs. Gary E. Johnson, the former governor of New Mexico, argues that legalizing drugs would "educate, regulate, tax, and control the estimated $400 billion a year drug industry."[12] Legalizing illicit drugs, Johnson asserts, would give the government much more control over drug usage and would end up leading to decreased drug use.

> "Cocaine use harms not only the addict but the cocaine user's family, fosters violence, and increases the chances of acquiring blood-borne diseases."

There are many drug policy experts who do not agree with legalization policies, however. They argue that such policies would just make it easier for addicts to abuse drugs and gives the appearance that the government sanctions drug use. John P. Walters, director of the Office of National Drug Control Policy, argues that drug "legalization, by removing penalties and reducing price, would increase drug demand. Make something easier and cheaper to obtain, and you increase the number of people who will try it." Walters dismisses the claim that allowing the government to produce and distribute drugs will reduce the dangers associated with illegal drugs. Prescription drugs such as OxyContin are regulated by the government, he contends, but nevertheless, prescription drug abuse is a serious problem. "The point is clear," Walters asserts. "The laws are not the problem."[13]

## What All Agree On

Whatever their stand on drug legalization, critics and supporters of the war on drugs agree that cocaine use harms not only the addict but the cocaine user's family, fosters violence, and increases the chances of acquiring blood-borne diseases such as HIV/AIDS and hepatitis C. While cocaine use is seen as a threat around the world, attempts to eliminate it have caused much controversy.

# Is Cocaine and Crack Addiction a Serious Problem?

> ❝We still cling to 20-year-old ideas that crack is somehow uniquely harmful: It is instantly addictive; it makes you especially violent; it causes women to abandon their babies; the babies of crack users will be basket cases. None of these are true.❞

—Eric E. Sterling, "Take Another Crack at That Cocaine Law."

> ❝It isn't solely that crack cocaine is in and of itself highly addictive that makes it such a devastating drug in our society; it's more that it acts as a turbo-charger on people who have addictive personalities.❞

—Will Self, "Lines, Damn Lines, and Statistics."

Cocaine users have been extolling the drug's exhilarating effects since the late 1800s when Sigmund Freud wrote *Über Coca* (*On Coca*), his "song of praise" for the drug.[14] A few years later he realized how dangerous the drug was when a good friend became addicted, and Freud soon joined the rest of society in condemning the drug.

## A Dangerous Drug

As Freud and his contemporaries eventually discovered, along with countless other users, researchers, and therapists since then, cocaine is a dangerous drug. The drug may not be physically addicting, but it is psychologically addicting. It gives the users intense feelings of euphoria and pleasure, unlike anything they have ever experienced before. A New Zealand–based drug information Web site explains the high this way:

> You'll feel a sudden burst of euphoria and self-confidence, be mentally alert, energized and buzzing. If you've been drinking a bit, you'll instantly wake up as if you were sober (but in a good way). You will be Mr. or Mrs. Sociable. . . . You'll probably feel like Superman on Viagra. Basically, coke temporarily turns you into a king-sized-sex-god (in your own mind, anyway).[15]

But unfortunately for cocaine users, the euphoric rush is short-lived. As users come down off the cocaine high, they experience a "crash," characterized by feelings of depression, fatigue, irritability, and dysphoria (the opposite of euphoria). So users crave the cocaine high again to feel the surge of pleasurable feelings they had been enjoying just a few minutes earlier. The realities of cocaine use are, however, that the user will never again feel the same intense euphoria they felt during their first high on cocaine. And furthermore, repeatedly using cocaine means that each high is a little bit lower than the previous high, and each crash is a little bit lower, until finally, one expert says, "Users not only report that they no longer feel high after cocaine use, but they report that cocaine use makes them feel paranoid and frightened. Despite the bad feelings, the compulsion to use cocaine not only persists but grows stronger over time with repeated use of the drug."[16]

> "The realities of cocaine use are, however, that the user will never again feel the same intense euphoria they felt during their first high on cocaine.

## Chasing the High

Robert Risinger, a researcher with the Medical College of Wisconsin discusses the phenomenon known as "chasing the high": "People often talk about 'chasing the high.' They abuse the drug several times in an episode, feel increasingly high with the first few hits, and experience a rapid dropoff in the duration of pleasure with repeated use—which may explain consuming larger amounts and more frequently over a session."[17]

Addicts discover that their craving for a cocaine high is satisfied for shorter and shorter periods of time before they have to have another dose. In time, addicts develop a tolerance to the drug; they have to use more and more cocaine in order to reach the same high. The New Zealand Web site describes the cocaine experience as: "Coke makes you feel good in short bursts, then goes bad on you. Even a single line comedown will make you feel edgy. You'll immediately want more. And more. And more."[18]

> **Animals in experiments with cocaine will pass up food, water, sex, and sleep for another hit of cocaine, until they die of hunger, dehydration, or exhaustion.**

Experiments with laboratory rats, mice, and monkeys found that the animals will self-administer cocaine to the exclusion of all other activities. They will press a bar hundreds or thousands of times hoping for just one dose of cocaine. Unlike in experiments with other addictive drugs, such as heroin, where the animals will take periodic breaks to eat or sleep, animals in experiments with cocaine will pass up food, water, sex, and sleep for another hit of cocaine, until they die of hunger, dehydration, or exhaustion.

## The Chemistry Behind the Cocaine High

The elation and the subsequent depression is due to the brain chemical known as dopamine. When a person has a rewarding experience—and the high from cocaine is definitely a pleasurable experience—dopamine is released in the nerve cells in the brain. Cocaine blocks the dopamine receptors on the nerve cells, however, which causes the dopamine to accumulate, leading to intense, euphoric feelings. The accumulated dopamine overloads the brain, which cannot sustain these intense, pleasurable feelings for long, and the user crashes. The result is that with regular and frequent drug use (addiction) or cocaine binges, the brain responds to the excess dopamine by reducing the amount of dopamine it normally produces. It also means that the brain requires higher and higher doses of cocaine to feel any sort of pleasure. The lower production of dopamine also makes it more difficult for the addict to get any pleasurable feelings out of formerly rewarding activities, which is why cocaine addicts often feel depressed, irritable, and fatigued when they are not high.

## Who Uses Cocaine?

According to the 2005 National Survey on Drug Use and Health, the number of past-month cocaine users has fluctuated between 0.8 and 1.0 percent of the population from 2002 to 2005, while the number of users in 2006 remains steady at 2.4 percent. And while the survey reports that the number of crack users increased from 467,000 in 2004 to 682,000 in 2005, the change in percentage (from 0.2 to 0.3 percent) is not statistically significant. The Drug Enforcement Administration reports that every year, between 5,000 and 7,000 people try cocaine for the first time, and of those new users, 25 percent become addicted. Others dispute those figures, claiming that the DEA's number of new cocaine users is inflated.

> **Cocaine addicts often feel depressed, irritable, and fatigued when they are not high.**

Cocaine use is most prevalent among adults aged 18 to 25, although the mean age of first use of cocaine is 19.7 years old, behind inhalants (16.1 years), PCP (16.5 years), marijuana (17.4 years), and LSD (18.3 years). Men are more likely to use cocaine than women. But among youths aged 12 to 18, boys and girls use cocaine in almost equal numbers. The disparity grows slightly among users 18 to 25, and by the time users are age 26 and older, nearly twice as many men use cocaine as women.

## Marijuana as a Gateway Drug

Studies have shown that many cocaine users used marijuana first before moving on to cocaine. Because of this, marijuana is often called a gateway drug, since it is said to lead users from one illicit drug to another. The National Institute on Drug Abuse asserts that the risk of trying cocaine is much greater for those who have tried marijuana. NIDA maintains that smoking marijuana exposes users to dealers and addicts of other drugs who may urge them to try harder drugs such as cocaine. Karen P. Tandy with the Drug Enforcement Administration, asserts that, "In drug law enforcement, rarely do we meet heroin or cocaine addicts who did not start their drug use with marijuana."[19]

Other researchers dispute these findings, however. Simply because a cocaine user also used marijuana before cocaine does not mean that marijuana caused the user to graduate to cocaine. A study by policy experts at the RAND Drug Policy Research Center found, "The people who are predisposed to use drugs and have the opportunity to use drugs are more likely than others to use both marijuana and harder drugs. Marijuana typically comes first because it is more available."[20]

## Addiction

While cocaine users do not experience the typical withdrawal symptoms of drug addiction, cocaine is an extremely addictive drug, psychologically if not physically. The American Psychiatric Association defines addiction as including at least three of the following symptoms: developing a tolerance for the drug; a withdrawal reaction when going without the drug; taking more of the drug and for longer periods than intended; wanting to or trying unsuccessfully to cut back on the amount of drugs taken; spending a great deal of time under the influence of the drug; giving up other activities and interests because of the drug; and using it despite its harmful physical or psychological effects.

While women are less likely to use cocaine, once they start using the drug, they are more likely to become addicted within two years. And although blacks comprise 11 percent of the U.S. population, they make up only 4 percent of new cocaine users. But despite these low numbers, blacks are nine times more likely than whites and Latinos to become addicted to cocaine during the first two years of use. Adolescents also face a greater risk of cocaine addiction; users who started abusing the drug in their late teens were more likely to become addicted to cocaine than those who started using after age 21.

> " Many cocaine users used marijuana first before moving on to cocaine. "

## Cocaine's Effects on the Body

One thing is clear to all who study and use cocaine—the drug has deleterious effects on the body. Snorting cocaine can cause the nose to collapse. The inside of the nose is covered by a thin mucous membrane filled with blood vessels. The membrane acts as a filter to protect the body against dust and other irritants—including cocaine—and also serves to humidify the air that is breathed in before it makes its way to the lungs. When cocaine is snorted through the nose, the blood vessels in the mucous membrane constrict and irritate and inflame the nose's lining. Symptoms of an irritated or inflamed nose include a runny nose, sneezing, nasal congestion, and nosebleeds. Cocaine can also permanently damage the membrane, leading to open sores on the membrane and perforation of the septum, the fleshy wall that separates the nose into two chambers. If cocaine abuse continues, the hole grows larger and larger until the septum collapses. Plastic surgery can improve the look of the nose but cannot reverse the damage.

Other studies have found more ways in which cocaine can damage the body. Cocaine users who share straws to snort cocaine may also be sharing the hepatitis C virus. Hepatitis C is a liver disease that is spread by contact with the blood of an infected person. There is no cure.

## Other Health Threats

Cocaine also is associated with a severe form of high blood pressure known as hypertensive crisis. The cocaine stimulates the heart and causes rapid heartbeats and increased cardiac functions. If the high blood pressure is severe or persistent, it can damage many of the body's vital organs such as the heart, brain, and kidney. Along with the high blood pressure, cocaine users also have an elevated risk of heart attack. Cocaine users are four times as likely to develop aneurysms—an abnormal bulge—in a coronary artery. While coronary artery aneurysms do not rupture as often as other types of aneurysms, they slow down the blood flow and can cause dangerous clots. Timothy D. Henry, a cardiologist with the Minneapolis Heart Institute, theorizes that cocaine's blood-constricting effects stress the user's blood pressure, which could lead to the aneurysm.

> " One thing is clear to all who study and use cocaine— the drug has deleterious effects on the body. "

Another study found a link between cocaine use and an elevated risk of developing Parkinson's disease. The cocaine appeared to alter nerve cells in the brain, making them more susceptible to the toxin that causes Parkinson's disease's symptoms. According to Richard Smeyne, the lead researcher and a neurobiologist at St. Jude's Children's Hospital, many former and current cocaine users are entering middle age when the disease makes its initial appearance. "It might not be surprising to see a rise in the number of cases of Parkinson's disease in the next ten or twenty years or so,"[21] he concludes.

## Differing Views

Even though most researchers, drug policy experts, and cocaine users themselves agree that cocaine is a dangerous drug, they differ on the seriousness of the addiction problem. Some cocaine users are able to use the drug recreationally a few times and stop using without any problem at all. Others use the drug once and are instantly addicted. In addition, some users seem to be able to escape any harmful effects of the drug while others unwittingly destroy their bodies. The differing views of cocaine will no doubt be debated for some time to come.

# Is Cocaine and Crack Addiction a Serious Problem?

**66The physiological and psychoactive effects of cocaine are similar regardless of whether it is in the form of powder or crack.99**

—Deborah J. Vagins and Jesselyn McCurdy, *Cracks in the System: Twenty Years of the Unjust Federal Crack Cocaine Law.* Washington, DC, 2006. www.aclu.org.

Vagins is the policy counsel for civil rights and civil liberties with the American Civil Liberties Union. McCurdy is the legislative counsel for the ACLU.

**66Crack is more potent and addictive, resulting in more emergency-room episodes and public-facility treatment admissions than powder cocaine, despite the fact that powder cocaine is more widely used.99**

—Alex Acosta, testimony before the U.S. Sentencing Commission, November 14, 2006.

Acosta is the U.S. attorney for the Southern District of Florida.

\* Editor's Note: While the definition of a primary source can be narrowly or broadly defined, for the purposes of Compact Research, a primary source consists of: 1) results of original research presented by an organization or researcher; 2) eyewitness accounts of events, personal experience, or work experience; 3) first-person editorials offering pundits' opinions; 4) government officials presenting political plans and/or policies; 5) representatives of organizations presenting testimony or policy.

**❝[Cocaine] is a deadly drug. . . . And it is horribly addictive.❞**

—Chellis Glendinning, "Cocaína No, Coca Si," April 12, 2006. www.alternet.org.

Glendinning is an author and psychologist who specializes in post-traumatic stress disorder.

---

**❝Up to 75% of people who try cocaine will become addicted to it.❞**

—Greater Dallas Council on Alcohol and Drug Abuse, "Cocaine: Statistics/Resources," March 31, 2005. www.gdcada.org.

The GDCADA develops campaigns to reduce alcoholism and drug abuse. The council also provides information to the public about intervention and preventing substance abuse.

---

**❝According to [Greater Dallas Council on Alcohol and Drug Abuse] statistics, 3,750 people become addicted to cocaine every day. Baloney.❞**

—Joseph Szydlowski, "Drug Policy Needs a Fix," *Northerner*, March 29, 2006.

Szydlowski was a student at Northern Kentucky University at the time this essay was published.

---

**❝No one ever feels *contented* after taking cocaine. They just want more.❞**

—Cocaine.org, "The Vials of Crack." www.cocaine.org.

Cocaine.org is an Internet-based information resource.

---

66 **Whereas powder cocaine tended to be used in private settings among more affluent people, crack was sold by and to a whole new class of people on inner-city street corners. In short, crack was a marketing innovation, not a new drug.** 99

—Craig Reinarman and Harry G. Levine, "Crack in the Rearview Mirror: Deconstructing Drug War Mythology," *Social Justice*, vol. 31, nos. 1–2, 2004.

Reinarman is a professor of sociology at the University of California in Santa Cruz. He has authored two books on cocaine, *Crack in America: Demon Drugs and Social Justice* (with Harry G. Levine), and *Cocaine Changes: The Experience of Using and Quitting*. Levine is a professor of sociology at Queens College, City University of New York, in Flushing.

66 **In very small and occasional doses [cocaine] is no more harmful than equally moderate doses of alcohol or marijuana, and infinitely less so than heroin.** 99

—James Inciardi, *The War on Drugs III: The Continuing Saga of the Mysteries and Miseries of Intoxication, Addiction, Crime, and Public Policy*. Boston: Allyn and Bacon, 2002.

Inciardi is the director of the Center for Drug and Alcohol Studies at the University of Delaware and a member of the Internal Policy Committee, Executive Office of the President, Office of the National Drug Control Policy. He has written numerous books in the areas of substance abuse, criminology, and public policy.

66 **Addicts don't tell the truth about their drug use. . . . We lie not because we are inherently dishonest people but because the nature of addiction is such that we have to lie in order to keep using and we have to keep using because our bodies literally need the drug to function.** 99

—William Cope Moyers, with Katherine Ketcham, *Broken: My Story of Addiction and Redemption*. New York: Viking, 2006.

Moyers, the son of journalist Bill Moyers, was himself a journalist who became addicted to cocaine. He went through recovery at the Hazelden Foundation, a rehabilitation center for alcoholics and drug addicts in Minnesota, and eventually became the vice president of external affairs at Hazelden.

66 Prolonged drug use changes the brain in fundamental and very long-lasting ways, and . . . those long-lasting changes persist long after you stop using the drug. . . . Prolonged cocaine use . . . changes the way in which the brain can use, in this case dopamine, for up to two years after an addict has stopped taking the drug. 99

—Alan I. Leshner, *ABC Forum,* November 24, 2005. www.abc.net.au.

Leshner, the former director of the National Institute on Drug Abuse, a federal agency that works to prevent drug abuse and addition, is the chief executive officer of the American Association for the Advancement of Science, the world's largest general science organization and publisher of the peer-reviewed journal *Science.*

66 Users like the feelings that drugs produce, and they believe they can get away with that use, that chemical high. 99

—Robert L. DuPont, *The Selfish Brain: Learning from Addiction.* Center City, MN: Hazelden, 2000.

DuPont is the president of the Institute for Behavior and Health in Rockville, Maryland, and a clinical professor of psychiatry at Georgetown University School of Medicine in Washington, D.C.

66 We have exceeded our two-year goal of reducing drug use among young people by 10 percent, and we are on track to reach our five-year goal [of reducing drug use by 25 percent]. 99

—George W. Bush, "National Drug Control Strategy Update 2005," February 2005. www.whitehousedrugpolicy.gov.

Bush is the forty-third president of the United States.

# Is Cocaine and Crack Addiction a Serious Problem?

- In 2004 more than **34 million** Americans aged 12 or older had used cocaine at least once in their lifetime, and 7.8 million reported using crack.

- In 2006, **2.5 percent** of all high school seniors had used cocaine in the past month, and **8.5 percent** had used cocaine in their lifetime.

- About **682,000** Americans used crack cocaine in 2005 compared to 2.4 million Americans who used powder cocaine.

- The Drug Enforcement Administration estimates that there are at least **5,000 to 7,000** new cocaine users in America every year, and at least **25 percent** will become addicted to cocaine within four years.

- Most cocaine is used in North America, which, with **6.5 million** users, accounts for almost half the global cocaine market.

- Women are **less likely** than men to start using cocaine, but once they start, they are three to four times **more likely** to become addicted within two years.

- In 2005 the average age of users who tried cocaine for the first time was **19.7 years old**.

- The 2006 National Drug Threat Survey found that **36.5 percent** of state and local agencies reported that cocaine was their greatest drug threat.

- While cocaine use is growing in Europe, the **United States** still has the highest consumption rate of cocaine in the world.

- Women who used cocaine and crack made up **17.1 percent** of admissions for illicit drug treatment in 2004.

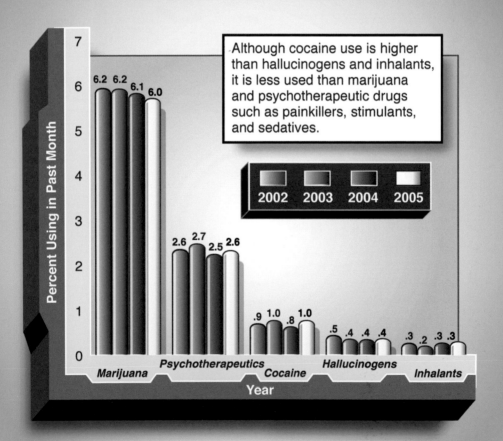

## Recent Illicit Drug Use Among Teens: 2002–2005

Although cocaine use is higher than hallucinogens and inhalants, it is less used than marijuana and psychotherapeutic drugs such as painkillers, stimulants, and sedatives.

2002  2003  2004  2005

Percent Using in Past Month

Marijuana: 6.2  6.2  6.1  6.0
Psychotherapeutics: 2.6  2.7  2.5  2.6
Cocaine: .9  1.0  .8  1.0
Hallucinogens: .5  .4  .4  .4
Inhalants: .3  .2  .3  .3

Year

Source: Substance Abuse and Mental Health Services Administration. (2005). *Overview of Findings from the 2004 National Survey on Drug Use and Health* (Office of Applied Studies, NSDUH Series H-27, DHHS Publication no. SMA 05–4061). Rockville, MD.

# How Cocaine Affects the Brain

In the normal communication process, dopamine is released by a neuron into the synapse, where it can bind with dopamine receptors on neighboring neurons. Normally, dopamine is then recycled back into the transmitting neuron by a specialized protein called a dopamine transporter. If cocaine is present, it attaches to the dopamine transporter and blocks the normal recycling process, resulting in a buildup of dopamine in the synapse, which contributes to the pleasurable effects of cocaine.

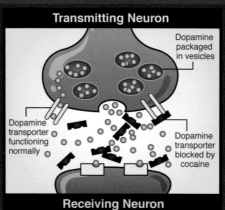

**Transmitting Neuron**

Dopamine packaged in vesicles

Dopamine transporter functioning normally

Dopamine transporter blocked by cocaine

**Receiving Neuron**

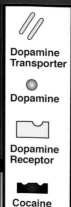

**Dopamine Transporter**

**Dopamine**

**Dopamine Receptor**

**Cocaine**

Source: National Institute on Drug Abuse, *Cocaine Abuse and Addiction*, November 2004.

# Use of Other Drugs Increases Exposure to Cocaine

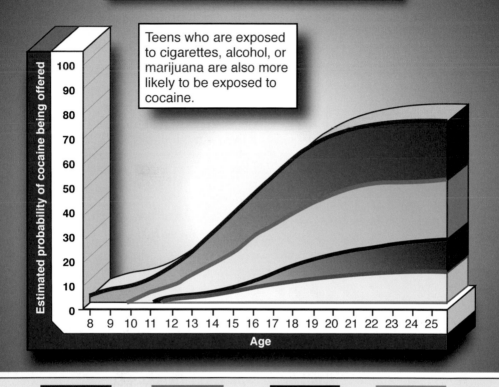

Teens who are exposed to cigarettes, alcohol, or marijuana are also more likely to be exposed to cocaine.

Alcohol/tobacco use and marijuana use started

No alcohol/tobacco use and no marijuana use

Alcohol/tobacco use but no marijuana use

No alcohol/tobacco use but marijuana use started

Source: Kimberly R. Martin, "Youth's Opportunities to Experiment Influence Later Use of Illegal Drugs," *NIDA Notes*, vol. 17, no. 5, January 2003.

- Cocaine is the most frequent cause of **drug-related deaths** reported by medical examiners and is the most commonly used illegal drug among people who are seeking medical care in hospital emergency rooms or drug treatment centers.

- Up to **33 percent** of cocaine users who thought they were healthy were actually infected with hepatitis C, a liver disease. There is no cure and no vaccine to prevent hepatitis C.

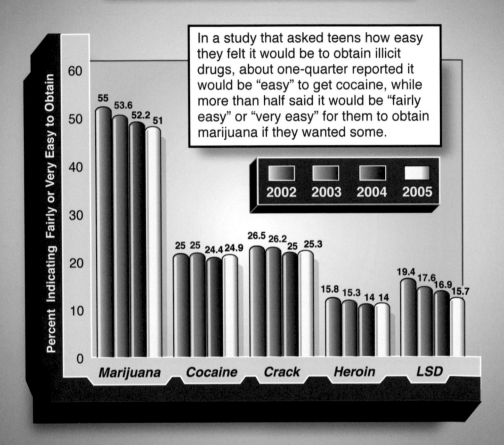

# Teens Reveal How Easy It Would Be to Obtain Cocaine

In a study that asked teens how easy they felt it would be to obtain illicit drugs, about one-quarter reported it would be "easy" to get cocaine, while more than half said it would be "fairly easy" or "very easy" for them to obtain marijuana if they wanted some.

2002  2003  2004  2005

Percent Indicating Fairly or Very Easy to Obtain

Marijuana: 55, 53.6, 52.2, 51
Cocaine: 25, 25, 24.4, 24.9
Crack: 26.5, 26.2, 25, 25.3
Heroin: 15.8, 15.3, 14, 14
LSD: 19.4, 17.6, 16.9, 15.7

Source: 2005 NSDUH: National Findings, SAMHSA Office of Applied Studies.

- Abusing cocaine could increase an individual's risk of developing **Parkinson's disease** later in life.

- Regular cocaine users are **four times** as likely to develop heart aneurysms.

- Researchers studying postmortem brain tissue samples found that cocaine harms the neurons that release **dopamine**, a neurochemical that regulates feelings of pleasure.

# Are Punishments for Cocaine and Crack Administered Fairly?

> **Higher penalties for crack cocaine offenses appropriately reflect the greater harm posed by crack cocaine.**
>
> —Alex Acosta, testimony before the U.S. Sentencing Commission.

> **The penalties for crack cocaine are unjust not just because they are more severe than those for powder cocaine, but also because the added severity doesn't make any sense.**
>
> —William D. McColl, "Federal Sentencing Laws: U.S. Sentencing Commission Testimony."

The emergence of crack cocaine in the mid-1980s revolutionized the illicit drug scene in the United States. Suddenly it became very inexpensive to achieve a euphoric drug high. A crack rock could be had for as little as five dollars. Cocaine was no longer reserved for celebrities like rock singers, sports stars, and the wealthy; now even the poor could fly high on cocaine by smoking crack. As the numbers of crack users skyrocketed, so, too, did violent crime, particularly gun violence and especially homicides among young black men. Harsh laws were passed in an attempt to crack down on crack use. Policy makers, social workers, and medical professionals decried the use of crack by pregnant women and predicted their babies would be permanently damaged by the mothers' prenatal cocaine use. Some public hospitals began to surreptitiously test pregnant, low-income women for cocaine, and a few women had their newborn babies taken away from them because they tested positive for the drug. In the decades since crack first appeared on the scene, America's prisons have been overflowing with low-level drug users, and new studies and grown-up "crack babies" are challenging long-held beliefs about the prenatal effects of crack on fetuses.

## Crack and Violent Crime

From 1984 to 1989, the homicide rate of black youths aged 14 to 17 doubled, while the homicide rate of black men aged 18 to 24 increased by a hefty 30 percent. The murder rate for black men aged 25 and over remained relatively flat, however, rising only 10 percent in this same time period. Murder rates for the general population did not follow the trend set by young black males, leading *Freakonomics* authors Steven D. Levitt and Stephen J. Dubner to attribute the increase in young black male homicides to the rise of crack cocaine in inner-city neighborhoods.

> Urban street gangs were the main distributors of crack cocaine. In the beginning, demand for their produce was phenomenal, and so were the potential profits. Most crack killings, it turns out, were not a result of some crackhead sticking up a grandmother for drug money but rather one crack dealer shooting another— and perhaps a few bystanders—in order to gain turf.[22]

> "The emergence of crack cocaine in the mid-1980s revolutionized the illicit drug scene in the United States."

The reason for the increase in violence was simple economics, they maintain.

Lawmakers responded to dramatic increase in crack-related crime by passing the Anti-Drug Abuse Act of 1986—legislation that mandated minimum prison sentences for crack and cocaine possession and distribution. Congress's intent was to target the major cocaine and crack dealers and traffickers, as shown in a 1986 report issued by the House Subcommittee on Crime on the proposed legislation. The subcommittee emphasized that "the Federal government's most intense focus ought to be on major traffickers . . . the heads of organizations, who are responsible for creating, and delivering very large quantities of drugs."[23]

# The 100:1 Sentencing Disparity

Administration officials, drug policy experts, and members of Congress concluded that crack—because of its almost instantaneous high—was a much more powerful drug than powdered cocaine, certainly psychologically addictive, and therefore much more dangerous to use than powdered cocaine. Deputy Attorney General Larry D. Thompson testified before the U.S. Sentencing Commission in March 2002 that crack cocaine is responsible for far more emergency room admissions than powdered cocaine, despite the fact that more users snort powdered cocaine than smoke crack. In addition, crack use is associated with violent crimes much more so than with other drugs. Twice as many crack convictions involve a weapon than powdered cocaine convictions. Crack addicts often commit robberies and assaults in order to finance their habit, and approximately one-third of female crack users turn to prostitution in order to get money to buy their drug.

> **Crack use is associated with violent crimes much more so than with other drugs.**

Furthermore, it was feared that due to its low cost and the ease in which it was manufactured and transported, crack use would soon become widespread. Senator Lawton Chiles of Florida explains why Congress decided to treat crack dealers more harshly:

> Those who possess five or more grams of cocaine freebase will be treated as serious offenders. Those apprehended with fifty or more grams of cocaine freebase will be treated as major offenders. Such treatment is absolutely essential because of the especially lethal characteristics of this form of cocaine. Five grams can produce 100 hits of crack. Those who possess such an amount should have the book thrown at them. The damage 100 hits can inflict upon users more than warrants this treatment.[24]

For this reason, Congress mandated that possession of five grams of crack would result in a five-year prison sentence, while it would require

500 grams of powdered cocaine—100 times the amount of crack need-ed—to earn the same sentence.

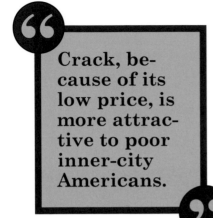

> Crack, because of its low price, is more attractive to poor inner-city Americans.

## The Racial Effect

Crack, because of its low price, is more attractive to poor inner-city Americans, many of whom are black, whereas powdered cocaine, a much more expensive drug, tends to be favored by more affluent suburbanites, many of whom are white. Law enforcement's emphasis on prosecuting crack offenses resulted in transforming American prisons into facilities filled with mostly black, low-level drug users. A 2005 report by the U.S. Sentencing Commission (USSC) found that 81 percent of crack defendants were black; and for 74 percent of convicted crack defendants and 87.2 percent of powdered cocaine defendants, no weapon was involved with their crime. A similar USSC report written in 2002 found that 73 percent of cocaine and crack defendants had a low-level involvement, such as street dealers, couriers, or lookouts.

## Attempts to Change the Mandatory Minimum Sentences

In the decades since Congress established the mandatory minimum sentences for crack and cocaine possession, numerous individuals and organizations, including judges, lawyers, social workers, drug policy experts, and the USSC (which was created by Congress in 1984 to determine fair and consistent prison sentences for all types of crimes), have concluded that crack and cocaine are essentially the same drug and that the sentencing disparity between the two drugs is unjustified. The USSC has recommended to Congress three times (in 1992, 1995, and 2002) that the amount of crack possessed by a drug offender be revised to a higher quantity before the mandatory minimum sentence is triggered. Its most recent recommendation was to change the cocaine-to-crack ratio to 20:1; possession of 25 grams of crack would result in a five-year mandatory prison sentence, while the amount of powder cocaine would remain at its current level of 500 grams for the same sentence. The USSC also urged that the mandatory minimum sentences for simple possession of crack cocaine be repealed.

Thompson and the U.S. Department of Justice rejected these suggested changes, however, arguing that crack cocaine devastates minority communities. "Lowering crack penalties would simply send the wrong message," Thompson testified, "that we care more about crack dealers than we do about the people and the communities victimized by crack. That is something that we simply cannot support."[25] In addition, urban crime is tied closely to crack use, as is risky sexual behavior. Instead of raising the thresholds for crack cocaine use, the DOJ recommends lowering the minimum quantity threshold for powdered cocaine.

In making the recommendations for the changes, the USSC noted that many of the beliefs that formed the basis of the mandatory minimum sentencing policy have been proven to be unfounded. For example, the homicide rate for black men has fallen since it peaked in 1989. Dubner and Levitt explain that "As demand fell, price wars broke out, driving down profits. And as the amount of money at stake grew smaller and smaller, the violence also dissipated. Young gang members are still selling crack on street corners, but when a corner becomes less valuable, there is less incentive to kill, or be killed, for it." And although the price of cocaine has fallen 75 percent from its peak, and while there are fewer crack users, Dubner and Levitt note that consumption still is about the same, which they say makes perfect sense. "If you are a devoted crackhead and the price is one-fourth what it used to be, you can afford to smoke four times as much."[26]

## Prenatal Cocaine Exposure

Another reason Congress supported the enhanced penalty for crack use was due to fears of a "crack baby" epidemic. The term *crack baby* first appeared in the mainstream media following a 1985 article in the *New England Journal of Medicine* written by Ira Chasnoff, a professor of pediatrics at the University of Illinois Medical School. Chasnoff and his colleagues compared a small group of women who used heroin,

> " Other studies have found that poverty, malnutrition, alcohol, and cigarette use during pregnancy have a greater effect on the fetus than does cocaine. "

methadone, and cocaine, and women who did not use any drugs at all during pregnancy. Their results showed that infants who had been exposed to drugs in utero were smaller, with a smaller head size, were more irritable, had difficulty focusing, and had feeding problems.

Some medical professionals, social workers, and even the media told of babies who were unimaginably tiny, mewled pathetically, could not stay still or be calm, and were always moving with jerky movements. Reporters and columnists said crack babies were a new "bio-underclass,"[27] who would suffer from severe, irreversible brain damage. "Crack babies," the articles claimed, would have barely functioning IQs and most likely be unable to care for themselves. Chasnoff never agreed with these predictions, which were later determined to be a gross exaggeration of what would befall the tiny infants. Other studies have found that poverty, malnutrition, alcohol, and cigarette use during pregnancy have a greater effect on the fetus than does cocaine.

## Follow-up Studies

However, prenatal cocaine exposure does have an effect on the developing minds of young children. Follow-up studies have shown that babies exposed prenatally to cocaine do experience problems later in life. Chasnoff and colleagues did follow-up studies when the babies were 2, 3, 4, 5, and 6 years old. They found that the children who had been prenatally exposed to cocaine had normal cognitive development at 2 years of age, and at 3 years, they had normal IQs. However, the researchers were starting to notice that the children were displaying behavioral problems starting as young as 3 years old. The children had problems with impulse control, distractions, and concentration, among others. They found that cocaine use did not affect cognitive development; the strongest factor on cognitive development was the family environment. If the mother continued to use drugs, the child was more likely to have cognitive problems. But surprisingly, Chasnoff and his fellow researchers also discovered that prenatal cocaine exposure was the most important factor in predicting behavioral problems.

> **Prenatal cocaine exposure was the most important factor in predicting behavioral problems.**

## Prenatal Cocaine Use and the Law

Despite the lack of evidence connecting a pregnant woman's cocaine use with her baby's well-being, many states enacted draconian drug laws. Hospitals in Charleston, South Carolina, began testing pregnant women for cocaine use in order to direct them into drug treatment programs. Later, the hospitals began giving the positive results to police, who tried to convince the women to get into treatment programs or face criminal charges. In 1988 the Medical University of South Carolina, alarmed by the apparent increase in cocaine use by pregnant women, began testing the urine of women suspected of being cocaine users. Women who tested positive were referred for counseling and treatment. Women who were more than 28 weeks into their pregnancy and who tested positive for cocaine use, however, were to be charged with "unlawful neglect of a child."[28] Ten women, including Crystal Ferguson, sued the City of Charleston and the hospital, claiming that the tests were unconstitutional searches. The case went all the way to the U.S. Supreme Court, which ruled in 2001 that the drug tests were indeed unconstitutional and that the tests had been performed without the women's knowledge or consent.

A second case also tested whether a woman could be prosecuted for using cocaine during her pregnancy. In *Whitner v. State of South Carolina*, Cornelia Whitner continued to use crack cocaine into her final trimester. She was charged with and convicted of criminal child neglect for using cocaine and sentenced to eight years in prison. She served 19 months before being released when the American Civil Liberties Union took over her case. Her conviction was overturned by a judge who ruled that child abuse charges could not be used for illicit drug use. The state appealed, however, and the South Carolina Supreme Court reversed the lower court's ruling. The court ruled that the fetus was indeed a "person" entitled to protection from criminal child neglect.

## The Law and Illicit Drug Use

As researchers study illicit drug use, the core beliefs about the need for draconian drug laws, drug testing, and the effects of crack and cocaine on adults and fetuses are being challenged. This chapter investigates some of the issues that legal advocates and opponents argue over, including the effectiveness of current crack and cocaine laws and theories about the impacts of prenatal cocaine use on the woman, her fetus, and society.

# Are Punishments for Cocaine and Crack Administered Fairly?

**❝Almost all federal crack prosecutions involve people of color.❞**

—Eric Sterling, "Take Another Crack at that Cocaine Law," *Los Angeles Times*, November 13, 2006.

Sterling is the president of the nonprofit Criminal Justice Policy Foundation in Silver Spring, Maryland, and served as counsel to the House Judiciary Committee, where his responsibilities primarily included antidrug legislation.

**❝The absence of a logical rationale for such a disparity [between crack and powder cocaine sentences] and its disproportionate impact on one historically disfavored race promotes disrespect for the law and suggests that the resulting sentences are unjust.❞**

—Gregory Presnell, *United States v. Jermaine Hamilton,* March 16, 2006.

Presnell is a judge at the U.S. District Court for the Middle District of Florida, Orlando Division.

Bracketed quotes indicate conflicting positions.

* Editor's Note: While the definition of a primary source can be narrowly or broadly defined, for the purposes of Compact Research, a primary source consists of: 1) results of original research presented by an organization or researcher; 2) eyewitness accounts of events, personal experience, or work experience; 3) first-person editorials offering pundits' opinions; 4) government officials presenting political plans and/or policies; 5) representatives of organizations presenting testimony or policy.

66 Crack cocaine is an especially dangerous drug, and its traffickers should be subject to significantly higher penalties than traffickers of like amounts of cocaine powder. 99

—Alex Acosta, testimony before the U.S. Sentencing Commission, November 14, 2006.

Acosta is a U.S. attorney for the Southern District of Florida and a former assistant attorney general for the Civil Rights Division of the Department of Justice.

66 Congress made it explicitly clear that in passing the current mandatory minimum penalties for crack cocaine, it intended to target 'serious' and 'major' drug traffickers. The opposite has proved true: mandatory penalties for crack cocaine offenses apply most often to offenders who are low-level participants in the drug trade. 99

—Deborah J. Vagins and Jesselyn McCurdy, *Cracks in the System.* Washington, DC: American Civil Liberties Union, October 2006.

Vagins is the policy counsel for civil rights and civil liberties for the ACLU; McCurdy is the legislative counsel for the ACLU.

66 The crack-baby epidemic . . . was a total fabrication. . . . What the cameras were capturing were the well-documented effects of malnutrition and poverty. 99

—Mike Gray, *Drug Crazy: How We Got into This Mess & How We Can Get Out.* New York: Random House, 1998.

Gray is a screenwriter and author of *Drug Crazy,* a book about the futility of the war on drugs.

**❝The prosecutions of pregnant women have focused on women who use illegal drugs despite the fact that many more children are at risk of harm from prenatal exposure to cigarettes and alcohol.❞**

—Lynn M. Paltrow, "Pregnant Drug Users, Fetal Persons, and the Threat to *Roe v. Wade*," *Albany Law Review*, 1999.

Paltrow is the executive director of the National Advocates for Pregnant Women in New York City.

---

**❝The 100-to-1 disparity in sentencing between crack cocaine and powder cocaine is not justifiable.❞**

—Jeff Sessions, "Sens. Sessions, Pryor, Cornyn and Salazar Introduce Drug Sentencing Reform Act," press release, July 25, 2006.

Sessions, a U.S. senator from Alabama and a former attorney general for Alabama, along with Senators Mark Pryor of Arkansas, John Cornyn of Texas, and Ken Salazar of Colorado, introduced the Drug Sentencing Reform Act of 2006 to reduce the disparity in sentencing between crack and powder cocaine from 100-to-1 to 20-to-1. The bill would reduce the penalty for crack cocaine and increase the penalty for powder cocaine.

---

**❝Medical researchers quickly discovered that it was extremely difficult to distinguish 'crack babies' from other babies born to similarly impoverished mothers.❞**

—Craig Reinarman and Harry G. Levine, "Crack in the Rearview Mirror: Deconstructing Drug War Mythology," *Social Justice*, January 2004.

Reinarman is a professor of sociology at the University of California at Santa Cruz, specializing in drug policy. Levine is a professor of sociology at Queens College, City University of New York, whose area of specialization is the sociology of drugs and alcohol. They are coauthors of two books on cocaine, *Crack in America: Demon Drugs and Social Justice* and *Cocaine Changes: The Experience of Using and Quitting.*

66 **Although prenatal cocaine exposure does not seem to affect most areas of cognitive function, the deficits in attention are consistent and lasting.** 99

—Barbara J. Strupp, quoted in Susan Lang, "Study Suggests Link Between Maternal Cocaine Use, Attention Dysfunction in Kids," *Cornell Chronicle,* June 15, 2000.

Strupp is an adjunct associate professor of psychology and an associate professor of nutritional science at Cornell University in Ithaca, New York. Her research specialty is human developmental cognitive disorders, such as how prenatal cocaine use affects the fetus.

66 **Our study found significant cognitive deficits with cocaine-exposed children twice as likely to have significant delay throughout the first 2 years of life.** 99

—Lynn T. Singer et al., "Cognitive and Motor Outcomes of Cocaine-Exposed Infants," *Journal of the American Medical Association,* April 17, 2002.

Singer, a professor of pediatrics and psychology at Case Western Reserve University in Cleveland, Ohio, is the lead researcher of a 2002 study on prenatal exposure to cocaine, which found that children exposed to cocaine in utero are more likely to experience problems in their cognitive developments.

66 **The quality of the caregiving environment appeared to have substantial compensatory effects on cocaine-exposed children placed in adoptive or foster care.** 99

—Lynn T. Singer et al., "Cognitive Outcomes of Preschool Children with Prenatal Cocaine Exposure," *Journal of the American Medical Association,* May 26, 2004.

Singer, a professor of pediatrics and psychology at Case Western Reserve University in Cleveland, Ohio, is the lead researcher of a 2004 study on prenatal exposure to cocaine. The study found that children up to age four who were exposed to prenatal cocaine use were less likely to develop above average IQs, but being raised in an adoptive or foster home could mitigate the outcomes for some children.

66 Even if cocaine is used only at the beginning of pregnancy and mother and infant are found to be free of cocaine at birth, the damage to the fetus has already occurred. 99

—Judith Schaffer, "Cocaine Use During Pregnancy: Its Effects on Infant Development and Implications for Adoptive Parents." www.nysccc.org.

Schaffer is the former Director of Family Resources for the Perinatal Cocaine Project for Birth, Foster, and Adoptive Families in New York City.

66 Cocaine is an illegal drug, but one whose use during pregnancy has been shown repeatedly does not necessarily lead to fetal harm—let alone the severe and lasting damage reported by a sensationalist press. The opposite situation exists with respect to fertility drugs, like Fertinex. . . . Here, the substantial likelihood of multiple pregnancies that place at grave risk both mother and babies is thoroughly documented in the professional literature. 99

—Lynn M. Paltrow, "Take Politics Out of Pregnancy," *Chicago Sun-Times,* July 12, 2001.

Paltrow is a civil liberties lawyer specializing in reproductive and health issues and the executive director for the National Advocates for Pregnant Women, an organization dedicated to protecting the rights of pregnant women and mothers.

66 Now, 10 years later, that kid who was called a 'crack baby' is in college about to get his associate's degree. 99

—Antwaun Garcia, "They Called Me a Crack Baby. So Why Am I in College?" *City Limits,* March 2004.

Garcia was born to a woman who used drugs during her pregnancy. He is now a writer for *Represent,* a magazine by and for teens in foster care.

# Facts and Illustrations

## Are Punishments for Cocaine and Crack Administered Fairly?

- A person convicted of possessing 5 grams of crack cocaine or 500 grams of powder cocaine receives a mandatory prison sentence of 5 years; **50 grams** of crack or **5,000 grams** of powder cocaine results in a mandatory 10-year-prison sentence.

- Since 1995 the U.S. Sentencing Commission has recommended more **equitable sentencing** for crack and powdered cocaine offenses. Congress, however, has rejected the commission's recommendations every time they have been presented.

- According to the Sentencing Project, the number of prisoners incarcerated in 2000 for drug use **equaled** the total number of inmates in prisons and jails in 1975.

- African Americans make up **15 percent** of the country's drug users, yet they comprise **37 percent** of those arrested for drug violations, **59 percent** of those convicted, and **74 percent** of those sentenced to prison for a drug offense.

- Women are the fastest-growing segment of the prison population, according to the **Women's Prison Association**, due mainly to mandatory minimum sentences for drug offenses. Statistics from the WPA show that the number of women arrested for drug offenses increased **37.5 percent** from 1995 to 2004, while males arrested for drug offenses increased only **23.3 percent**.

## In Cocaine Trade, Street Dealers Most Likely to Be Prosecuted

The federal sentencing laws Congress passed in the 1980s were intended to impose tough sentences on high-level drug market operators, such as manufacturers, heads of organizations distributing large quantities of narcotics, and serious traffickers with a substantial drug-trade business. However, the U.S. Sentencing Commission found that crack cocaine penalties apply most often to offenders who perform low-level trafficking functions, wield little decision-making authority, and have limited responsibility.

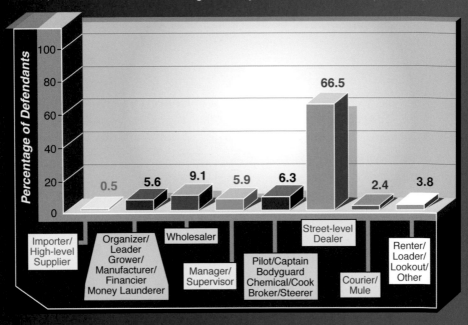

Source: The Sentencing Project, "Federal Crack Cocaine Sentencing," February 2007. www.sentencingproject.org.

- According to a **10-year study of children** exposed to drugs in the womb by Deborah Frank, newborns exposed in utero to heroin or methadone are indistinguishable from children exposed to cocaine or crack.

- Cocaine use in pregnant women can cause **spontaneous abortion** (38 percent); separate the placenta lining from the uterus (2 to 15 percent); and cause an increased incidence of **stillbirths** as the result of the implantation of the placenta near the top of the cervix (8 percent).

- A group of **30 leading medical doctors**, psychological experts, and scientists released an open letter to the media in February 2004 asking reporters and journalists to stop using the term *crack baby*, as they say it is pejorative, stigmatizes the child, and there is no recognizable syndrome, condition, or disorder that it represents.

- The Maryland Court of Appeals ruled in *Kilmon v. State* in August 2006 that women who use **cocaine while pregnant** cannot be prosecuted for reckless endangerment of the children they are carrying.

## Cocaine Use and Pregnancy

A study supported by the National Institute on Drug Abuse was able to separate the effects of prenatal maternal cocaine use from those of poor prenatal care and maternal use of other drugs. The study found that children born to poor, urban women who used cocaine throughout pregnancy were more likely to have significant cognitive defects during their first two years of life as children with similar backgrounds but no prenatal cocaine exposure.

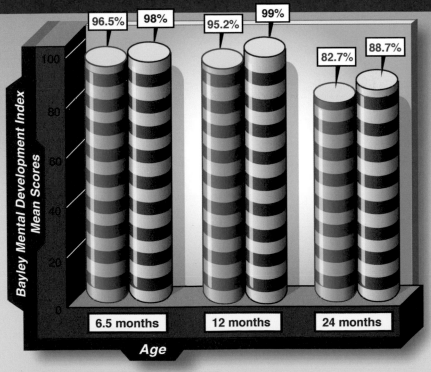

Source: *NIDA Notes*, vol. 17, no. 5, January 2003.

## Crack Cocaine Gets Longest Average Prison Sentences

The U.S. Sentencing Commission compiled statistics on the average prison sentence for simple possession and for more serious drug offenders who were convicted of drug trafficking, drug possession near schools or other protected locations, participating in a criminal drug enterprise with five or more individuals, or renting or managing a drug establishment. Crack cocaine had the highest average prison sentence at around 120 months.

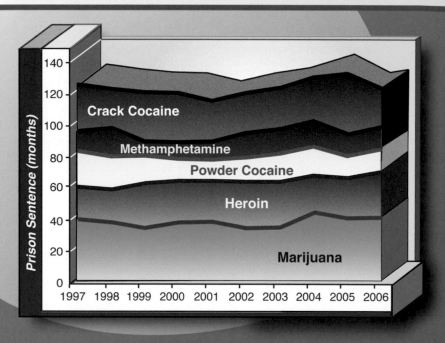

Source: U.S. Sentencing Commission, 1997–2006 Datafiles, USSCFY 97-USSCFY 06.

- **Cocaine-exposed infants**, especially those exposed near birth, have been found to be more irritable, jittery, and have interrupted sleep patterns, visual disturbances, and an inability to deal appropriately with sensory stimulation. Some of these complications may last 8 to 10 weeks after birth or even longer.

# Cocaine Prison Sentences by Race

Drug use rates are similar among all racial and ethnic groups. For all drug use, two-thirds of users in the United States are white or Hispanic. Despite these facts, blacks are disproportionately subject to the penalties for crack cocaine. Indeed, 81 percent of crack cocaine users sentenced in 2005 were black.

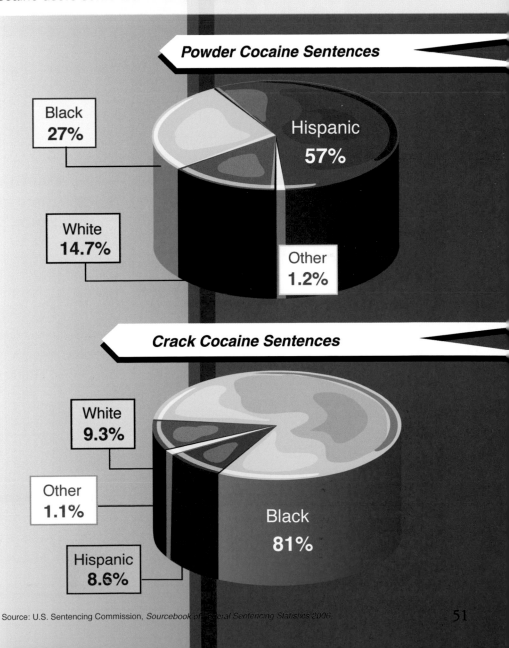

**Powder Cocaine Sentences**

Black
**27%**

Hispanic
**57%**

White
**14.7%**

Other
**1.2%**

**Crack Cocaine Sentences**

White
**9.3%**

Other
**1.1%**

Hispanic
**8.6%**

Black
**81%**

Source: U.S. Sentencing Commission, *Sourcebook of Federal Sentencing Statistics 2006.*

51

# How Should Cocaine and Crack Addiction Be Treated?

66 It is far from clear that coerced clients move closer to therapeutic objectives because of longer stays in treatment. 99

—Stephen Norland, Robin E. Sowell, and Albert DiChiara, "Assumptions of Coercive Treatment: A Critical Review."

66 A drug court's coercive power is the key to admitting drug-involved offenders into treatment quickly, for a period of time that is long enough to make a difference. 99

—National Drug Court Institute, "Drug Court Benefits."

Cocaine provides such a euphoric—albeit very short—high that it is very difficult to forget. Users seek to re-create that first cocaine high by taking another dose and then another, which is what often leads them into trouble—abuse, and sometimes addiction. Addicts who want to overcome their addiction have several treatment options, although opinions vary on whether the addict has to want to get sober or whether a coercive treatment plan is effective.

## What Is Addiction?

As crack and cocaine users slide past abuse to dependence and finally into addiction, there are signs, both subtle and obvious, that they are developing problems with drugs. Most addicts follow the same pattern, starting first with experimenting with crack or cocaine, then depending on it to give them an extra boost to overcome a stressful or unhappy situation, until finally they are psychologically addicted to the drug. They feel the need to take the drug in order to feel good.

But the problem with cocaine addiction is that the longer a person uses the drug, the less effective the drug is in giving the user a high. Users develop a physical tolerance to the drug and so they need to take more and more cocaine to get high, but the high is never as exhilarating as it once was. The crash after the high lasts longer, too, and the users often feel depressed and are unable to feel any sort of pleasurable feelings when they are not taking the drug. In addition, they feel edgy, nervous, anxious, fatigued, and paranoid, even when they are not experiencing a cocaine crash.

## Symptoms of Cocaine Addiction

It can sometimes be difficult to determine if a cocaine user is an addict. Some users may get addicted to cocaine immediately, even after just one use, while for others addiction can come on gradually. Although an increase in the amount and the frequency of use are clear signs that a user may have developed an addiction, there are other signs that indicate a cocaine abuse problem. Addicts can no longer use the drug in moderation; every time they abuse cocaine they do so until they have run out of drugs, are out of money to buy more drugs, or until they are physically unable to use more cocaine.

Another symptom of addiction is a change in the user's attitudes and priorities toward activities and interests that used to be important. Thoughts about family, friends, school or work, and hobbies are now replaced by thoughts of acquiring and using cocaine. Cocaine addicts constantly crave the drug and are completely preoccupied with getting and using more.

> **Addicts feel the need to take the drug in order to feel good.**

Some of the behaviors that may signal an addiction to cocaine include using at inappropriate times, such as before going to work or school, or driving; missing work or school because of cocaine use; decreased work or school performance; problems with family, friends, coworkers, classmates, or teachers due to drug use; stealing from family, friends, or coworkers; secretive or defensive behavior; abrupt mood changes or temper outbursts; change in hygiene habits; and loss of interest in hobbies, interests, and favorite pastimes.

Addiction alters both brain chemistry and behavior. What would once have been unthinkable behavior for the addict now seems completely natural. For example, when one mother of an addict questioned her daughter about her decision to live in her car (after being evicted from her apartment for nonpayment of rent and selling off most of her possessions in order to buy more drugs), the daughter told her that "a lot of people live in their cars" and it was "not a big deal."[29]

## Denial

Family and friends may see the change in the addict but not understand what is happening until one day they realize the addict is not at all the person they know and love. The addict has changed and become a stranger whose values and beliefs and even personality are gone. Not only are friends and family members often in denial about a loved one's addiction, but so is the addict. When confronted with their addiction, addicts will deny they have a problem and insist they can quit using drugs any time they want. Often the addict will accuse the accuser of having the problem, of imagining things or making things seem worse than they are. According to Beverly Conyers, author of *Addict in the Family: Stories of Loss, Hope, and Recovery*, "Denial is the foundation of addiction, the fertile soil in which it grows and flourishes. Denial provides the comforting delusion that everything is all right." Conyers goes on to say that addicts "will always deny their addiction, or, if forced to admit it, they will minimize its depth."[30]

> **The problem with cocaine addiction is that the longer a person uses the drug, the less effective the drug is in giving the user a high.**

## Treating Cocaine Addiction Medically

Unlike heroin, which can be treated with an alternative drug, methadone, there are no drugs that are currently used to treat cocaine addiction. There are a few promising anti-addiction drugs, such as AME-359, being used in clinical trials, however. The drugs being developed work in ways that are similar to vaccines; a small portion of a cocaine molecule is attached to a carrier molecule in the vaccine. When the user is injected with the vaccine, the body develops "antibodies" to cocaine. A user who has been injected with the cocaine vaccine will not get high from cocaine use, because the antibodies will attach themselves to the cocaine molecules, making them too large to pass through the bloodstream barrier. The theory is that if the user does not derive any pleasure from using cocaine, he or she will stop using it. Researchers also say AME-359 could be an antidote for cocaine overdoses. Laboratory rats who were given the vaccine and then given a cocaine overdose all survived, whereas rats who were not given the vaccine prior to the cocaine overdose all died.

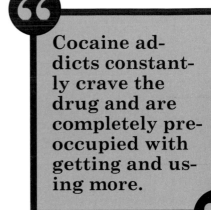

"Cocaine addicts constantly crave the drug and are completely preoccupied with getting and using more."

Disulfiram, also known by its trade name Antabuse, is also being tested with cocaine addiction. Disulfiram interferes with the metabolism of cocaine, preventing the user from feeling the euphoric high associated with the drug. Instead of a cocaine high, users experience the negative feelings associated with a cocaine crash, such as anxiety, restlessness, and paranoia. According to Richard Schottenfeld, a physician at Yale University Medical School, "If a patient on disulfiram slips and uses cocaine, the medication may make cocaine's effects so unpleasant they deter further use."[31] But while disulfiram may help addicts kick their cocaine habit, studies have found that disulfiram used in combination with therapy programs is even more effective in treating cocaine addiction.

## Behavioral Treatment Programs

Because every drug addict is different, treatment programs must be tailored to fit each individual. What works for one addict may not be effective with another addict. That said, the most common and effective treatment programs are behavioral therapy programs, of which two are most often used: interpersonal psychotherapy (IPT) and cognitive behavioral therapy (CBT). Both therapies can be used for a relatively short term (12 weeks, although longer programs are even more effective), and both can be used as either in-patient or out-patient programs.

> **Addiction alters both brain chemistry and behavior.**

Addicts who are experiencing problems in other areas of their personal lives are often referred to interpersonal psychotherapy. The goal of interpersonal psychotherapy is to not only help users recover from addiction, but to help addicts stop using drugs as a crutch to cope with the problems in their lives. According to IP therapists, drug abuse is "a dysfunctional attempt to cope with interpersonal problems."[32] The goal of the IP therapist is to help the addict find better ways to deal with personal problems. For example, if the addict is unemployed, the therapist may help with vocational training or career counseling. If the user is experiencing marital problems, the addict and his or her spouse may need couples counseling.

## Cognitive Behavioral Therapy

Cognitive behavioral therapy (CBT) uses a slightly different approach to treat cocaine addiction. Cocaine cravings are often triggered by cues— thoughts, sensory cues, situations, and behaviors. For example, the addict may think about the pleasurable feelings of a cocaine high (while denying the unpleasant aspects of use); or the addict may see, hear, smell, touch, or taste something that reminds him or her of cocaine. Situations the drug user encountered on a regular basis while using cocaine, as well as rituals associated with drug use, may trigger an intense craving for cocaine. Cognitive behavioral therapy, also known as relapse prevention, helps addicts recognize, avoid, and cope with these cocaine triggers. CBT helps addicts recognize situations in which they are most likely to encounter or use cocaine, avoid those situations, and cope more effectively with the problems associated with cocaine abuse. Addicts are also taught new ways to see and respond to their environment, along with skills to refuse cocaine.

Studies have found that when behavioral therapy programs are combined with disulfiram treatment, they are more effective in treating cocaine abuse than either therapy or medication alone. CBT and disulfiram have been found to be a more effective therapy program than IPT and disulfiram. Because addiction is considered a brain disease, relapse should not be unexpected. Just as other diseases experience relapse, so, too, does cocaine addiction. One study found that the relapse rate for cocaine addicts was less than 50 percent. "Relapse rates for treatment of alcohol, opioids and cocaine are less than those for hypertension and asthma, and equivalent to those of diabetes, all chronic conditions."[33] A study with laboratory mice found that cocaine permanently changed the neural connections in the brain, leading researchers to conclude that even after a long period of abstinence from cocaine, users may be prone to relapse.

## Drug Courts

Many cocaine addicts enter treatment programs through drug courts. Drug courts are a relatively new program in which nonviolent drug offenders, usually first- or second-time offenders, are sent to treatment programs instead of being incarcerated. Drug offenders go through treatment programs, undergo regular drug testing, are continually supervised, and receive legal sanctions if they break the terms of their drug court treatment program. Those who go through drug court programs are supervised by judges; prosecuting and defense attorneys; law enforcement personnel; educational; vocational; and community leaders; and counselors and therapists. Supporters of drug court programs maintain that sending nonviolent drug offenders to drug courts ensures that prisons are filled with violent offenders rather than nonviolent drug users.

Some debate has arisen over whether addiction therapy is more effective when the drug user enters the program voluntarily or is forced to participate, such as through drug courts. Several studies have found that drug users who were forced to participate in drug court treatment programs benefited as much as, or even more than, drug users who entered treatment programs voluntarily. There are two main

> " A user who has been injected with the cocaine vaccine will not get high from cocaine use. "

reasons for this result: The longer a drug user stays in treatment, the better the chances are the user can stay off drugs. Secondly, users who enter treatment through drug courts generally stay in treatment longer than those who enter treatment voluntarily.

## Treatment Is Cost-Effective

Numerous studies have found that treating cocaine addiction is much cheaper and more cost effective than imprisoning the cocaine or crack addict. A RAND Corporation study found that a dollar spent treating a cocaine addict saves society $7.50 in terms of the costs of arresting and incarcerating drug offenders, and the subsequent savings incurred when the drug user leaves treatment, becomes a productive member of society again, and leaves a life of crime.

The savings could be quite substantial. For the fiscal year 2006, 11,464 people were arrested and sentenced for federal cocaine offenses. At an estimated average of $20,000 per inmate per year for incarceration, those cocaine addicts cost the country more than $229 million. Treatment for those same 11,464 cocaine abusers, at an estimated cost of $4,500 per abuser, would cost just over $51.5 million, a savings of $177.5 million per year. In 2005, 256,491 people entered treatment for cocaine abuse. Cocaine abuse accounted for 13.9 percent of all substance abuse treatment admissions.

## A Difficult Drug to Treat

Because of cocaine's intense high and potential for addiction, cocaine addiction is very difficult to treat successfully. Addicts often suffer relapses, frequently more than once. A smell, a sight, a sound, a location, or even being in the presence of old cocaine-using buddies can trigger strong cravings for the drug. Different treatments for cocaine addiction are offered, and both addicts and society are benefiting from them.

# How Should Cocaine and Crack Addiction Be Treated?

"Addiction to cocaine, at least in mice, can happen much more quickly than previously thought. Mice . . . stayed addicted to cocaine for nearly a year after only one dose of the drug."

—Kristen Philipkoski, "Designing Drugs to Swat Addiction," *Wired,* March 29, 2004. www.wired.com.

Philipkoski is a freelance writer.

.................................................................................................................................

"There's a myth out there that you have to want drug treatment in order for it to work. That's not true."

—Alan I. Leshner, *Frontline: Drug Wars,* October 10, 2000.

Leshner, former director of the National Institute on Drug Abuse, a federal agency that works to prevent drug abuse and addition, is the chief executive officer of the American Association for the Advancement of Science, the world's largest general science organization and publisher of the peer-reviewed journal *Science.*

.................................................................................................................................

* Editor's Note: While the definition of a primary source can be narrowly or broadly defined, for the purposes of Compact Research, a primary source consists of: 1) results of original research presented by an organization or researcher; 2) eyewitness accounts of events, personal experience, or work experience; 3) first-person editorials offering pundits' opinions; 4) government officials presenting political plans and/or policies; 5) representatives of organizations presenting testimony or policy.

**❝Getting sober is a personal thing ... and no drug treatment program can help you beat addiction if you're not ready to play an active role in the fight.❞**

—Cliffside Malibu, "Drug Treatment Information 3/19," March 19, 2007. www.drugtreatmentinformation.com.

Cliffside Malibu is a residential rehabilitation and treatment center for adults suffering from alcoholism, drug addiction, eating disorders, depression, and other co-occurring disorders.

**❝It is clear that drug abusers do not respond to imprisonment. In some studies, over 95 percent of drug-abusing offenders returned to drug use within three years of their release from prison, with the lion's share [85 percent] relapsing within only the first six to 12 months.❞**

—David S. DeMatteo, Douglas B. Marlowe, and Davis S. Festinger, "A Sober Assessment of Drug Courts," *Federal Sentencing Reporter,* vol. 16, no. 2, December 2003.

DeMatteo and Festinger are research scientists in the Law and Ethics Research section at the Treatment Research Institute at the University of Pennsylvania. Marlowe is the director of law and ethics research at TRI. Festinger and Marlowe are also adjunct associate professors of psychiatry at the University of Pennsylvania School of Medicine.

**❝Treatment instead of incarceration would enhance public safety by reducing drug-related crime and preserving jail and prison space for violent offenders.❞**

—Drug Policy Alliance New Mexico, "Treatment for Drug Possession Arrestees: Frequently Asked Questions," revised, January 15, 2007. www.improvenewmexico.org.

The members of the Drug Policy Alliance believe that the war on drugs is doing more harm than good. It works to change drug policies so that nonviolent drug users are no longer arrested or incarcerated.

**66** Treatment is also much cheaper than enforcement in that it costs much less to run a heavy user through treatment than it does to incarcerate a seller (or the user).**99**

—Jonathan P. Caulkins et al., *How Goes the 'War on Drugs? An Assessment of U.S. Drug Programs and Policy.* Santa Monica, CA: RAND, 2005.

Caulkins has written numerous articles and monographs on drug policy and drug treatment options for the RAND Corporation. He chairs the Office of National Drug Control Policy's Data, Research, and Evaluation Committee and is on the Social Marketing Advisory Board for Drug Free America.

**66** Dollar for dollar, treatment reduces the societal costs of substance abuse more effectively than incarceration does.**99**

—Doug McVay, Vincent Schiraldi, and Jason Ziedenberg, "Treatment or Incarceration? National and State Findings on the Efficacy and Cost Savings of Drug Treatment Versus Imprisonment," *Justice Policy Institute Policy Report,* March 2004.

McVay is the research director and projects coordinator for Common Sense for Drug Policy, a nonprofit policy research organization based in Falls Church, Virginia. Schiraldi is the former executive director of the Justice Policy Institute in Washington, D.C., a think tank that researches pressing criminal and juvenile justice issues. Ziedenberg is the executive director of JPI.

**66** Statistics show that drug courts are a success, yet Congress persists in mandating ever stiffer sentences for federal offenders who need treatment more than punishment.**99**

—Donald P. Lay, "Rehab Justice," *New York Times,* November 18, 2004.

Lay, a distinguished professor of law at William Mitchell College of Law in St. Paul, Minnesota, was a former senior judge for the U.S. Court of Appeals for the Eighth Circuit.

66 Thinking out of the box means helping substance abusers, and ultimately society, by not viewing abstinence as the be all and end all of addiction treatment. There are many roads to recovery, and harm reduction is a promising addition to the treatment continuum. 99

—Howard Josepher, "Drug Treatments Needs a Shot in the Arm," *New York Nonprofit Press,* June 2006.

Josepher is the director of Exponents, a nonprofit organization dedicated to improving the quality of life of those affected by drug addiction, incarceration, and HIV/AIDS. It offers programs to help drug addicts traverse the stages of addiction to recovery.

66 [Cognitive-behavioral treatment] attempts to help patients recognize, avoid, and cope; i.e., recognize the situations in which they are most likely to use cocaine, avoid these situations when appropriate, and cope more effectively with a range of problems and problematic behaviors associated with drug use. 99

—National Institute on Drug Abuse, "Cocaine: Abuse and Addiction," revised, *Research Reports,* November 2004.

The National Institute on Drug Abuse is a federal agency that supports research on drug abuse issues and then ensures the rapid and effective dissemination of the results of the research to improve prevention, treatment, and policy options as they relate to drug abuse.

66 A complete change of environment, especially a holiday in the company of supportive family and (drug-free) friends, can help break a user's self-destructive cycle of coke-binges. The brain is given time to recover. 99

—Cocaine.org, "How to Quit Cocaine." http://cocaine.org.

Cocaine.org is a Web site that lists the history of and facts about crack and powdered cocaine.

# Facts and Illustrations

## How Should Cocaine and Crack Addiction Be Treated?

- A study cited in a Lancet article by C.P. P'Brien found the relapse rate for cocaine addicts was less than **50 percent**.

- A RAND Corporation study found that each dollar spent on treatment for cocaine addicts saves society up to **$7.50** by reducing crime costs and turning a drug user into a productive member of society.

- Cocaine abuse accounted for **13.9 percent** of all substance abuse treatment.

- From 1995 to 2005, the number of admissions to treatment for cocaine decreased from **278,421** in 1995 to **256,491** in 2005.

- According to a 2003 study on drug courts in New York State by the Center for Court Innovation, the reconviction rate among **2,135 offenders** who participated in 6 of the state's drug courts averaged 29 percent lower (ranging from 13 to 47 percent) over 3 years than for offenders who did not enter drug courts.

- Drug treatment in prison yields a benefit of between $1.91 and $2.69 for every dollar spent on programs. By contrast, community-based drug treatment programs generated **$3.30 of benefit** for every dollar spent.

- Of the users who were admitted for treatment in 2005, **72 percent** of those who primarily used cocaine used crack cocaine.

- The number of crack users who were admitted for treatment declined from **207,608 users** (12.4 percent of drug treatment admissions) in 1995 to 185,236 (10.0 percent) in 2005.

# Drug Court Expansion

The first drug court was established in 1989 in Miami, Florida, and has since grown to nearly 1,800 drug courts in all 50 states by the end of 2006. Drug courts are an innovative approach to getting substance abusers into treatment. Drug courts use legal sanctions and support from family, friends, and counselors to help users get and stay sober. Studies have found that within the first year of release, 43.5 percent of drug offenders are rearrested, whereas only 16.4 percent of drug court graduates are rearrested.

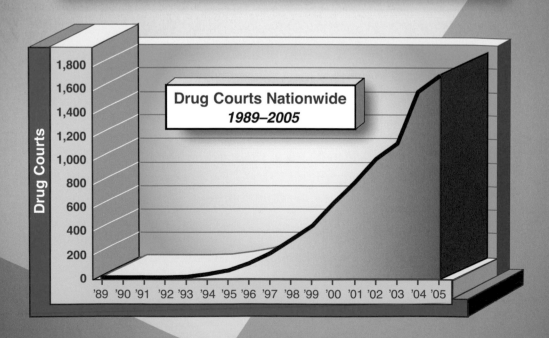

**Drug Courts Nationwide**
*1989–2005*

Source: *National Drug Control Strategy*, February 2006.

## Reducing Cocaine Abuse

During the course of a 12-week study, patients taking disulfiram or participating in cognitive-behavioral therapy (CBT) demonstrated greater reductions in cocaine abuse than those taking a placebo (sugar pill) or receiving interpersonal psychotherapy (IPT).

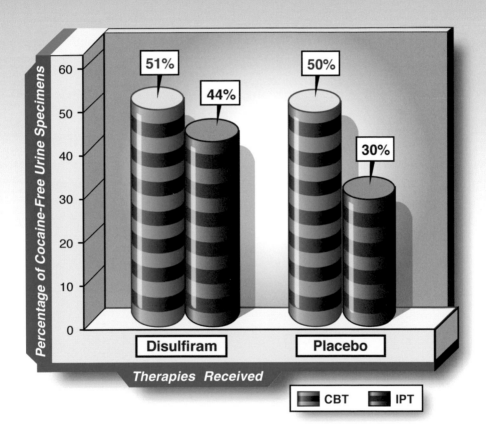

Source: Lori Whitten, "Disulfiram Reduces Cocaine Abuse," *NIDA Notes,* vol. 20, no. 2, August 2005.

- Of those users who were admitted to treatment for smoking cocaine in 2004, **53 percent were black**, 38 percent were white, and 7 percent were Hispanic. For powdered cocaine, **29 percent were black**, 51 percent were white, and 16 percent were Hispanic.

- A 2004 study found that femail cocaine addicts did not respond as well to treatment with disulfiram as male addicts. While **49 percent** of male addicts treated with disulfiram stayed sober (compared to 30 percent of male addicts who were given a placebo), **38 percent** of female addicts treated with disulfiram stayed sober, compared to **39 percent** of female addicts who were given a placebo.

- According to a U.S. government report that tracks treatment admissions in the United States, almost **32 percent** of all patients admitted for drug or alcohol treatment in 2005 were women. Of these women, **13 percent** primarily abused crack cocaine; **4.1 percent** reported abusing powder cocaine.

## Cost of Imprisonment Versus Cost of Treatment

Incarcerating drug offenders is much more expensive than treating them for their drug problems. The average cost of a year in prison is $27,000, compared to a year of treatment, $4,500. States could save $22,500 per year per drug offender by treating them rather than imprisoning them. In addition, for every dollar spent by government on treatment, it saves $7 in other costs (lower crime rates, health problems, and criminal justice costs).

$27,000

$4,500

**Cost of Incarceration**     **Cost of Treatment**

Source: Substance Abuse, Mental Health Services Administration, *Facts in a Flash 2002*.

# Risk of Relapse

The chronic nature of drug addiction means that not only is relapsing possible, it is likely. Diabetes, hypertension, and asthma are all chronic medical illnesses that require behavior modification. Relapse does not mean that treatment has failed.

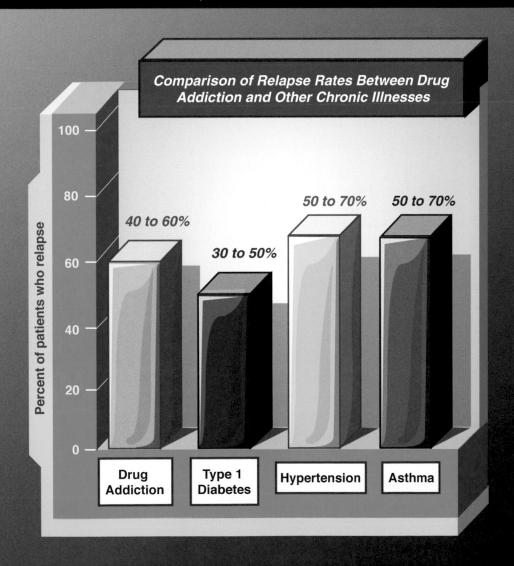

**Comparison of Relapse Rates Between Drug Addiction and Other Chronic Illnesses**

Percent of patients who relapse

- Drug Addiction: 40 to 60%
- Type 1 Diabetes: 30 to 50%
- Hypertension: 50 to 70%
- Asthma: 50 to 70%

Source: National Institute on Drug Abuse, *Drugs, Brains, and Behavior: The Science of Addiction*, 2007.

# Is the War on Cocaine Effective?

66 As long as there is demand, there will be supply. . . . [Politicians] also know . . . it is political suicide to admit this and propose policies that accept illegal drug use as inevitable. 99

—Robin Kirk, *More Terrible than Death: Massacres, Drugs, and America's War in Colombia.*

66 The significant declines in drug use since the President took office show that, with effective policy combining enforcement, treatment, and prevention, . . . real advances are possible. 99

—Office of National Drug Control Policy, *National Drug Control Strategy Update.*

The United States wages its war against cocaine on three fronts: smuggling interdiction, intercepting cocaine shipments as they enter the United States; eradication, spraying coca plants with weed killer, pulling the bushes out by hand, or convincing the peasants who grow coca bushes to switch to other crops; and education and treatment, educating Americans about the dangers of drug use and how to get treatment. Despite these efforts, though, every year the amount of coca bushes eradicated increases, the amount of cocaine seized in drug busts increases—and the number of users seeking treatment increases. Cocaine continues to remain plentiful and easily available in the United States.

## An Ideal Location

The coca bush, *Erythroxylon coca*, from which cocaine is made, is grown in South America. Between 80 and 90 percent of the world's cocaine is produced in Colombia. Bolivia and Peru supply the rest of the world's cocaine. Coca bushes used to be grown on huge plantations, but due to eradication efforts by Colombia and the United States, farmers have started growing the bushes on smaller plots hidden by thick jungle growth. After the leaves are harvested, they are transported to remote laboratories, usually in southern Colombia, where they are transformed into cocaine using many hazardous and toxic chemicals such as gasoline or kerosene, hydrochloric or sulfuric acid, and acetone or ether. The end product is cocaine hydrochloride, a crystalline powder that is 99 percent pure cocaine.

Colombia is ideally located to smuggle cocaine into the United States. It has coasts on both the Caribbean Sea and the Pacific Ocean and is connected to Central America by the Isthmus of Panama. Seaports, airports, and land routes north are all convenient and easily accessible for smugglers. Drug cartels, loosely organized networks of drug traffickers, are based in the cities of Cali, Medellín, and Bogotá, and are responsible for smuggling cocaine north. Approximately 90 percent of the cocaine smuggled into the United States enters via Mexico.

> **Approximately 90 percent of the cocaine smuggled into the United States enters via Mexico.**

The U.S. government's main focus is on smuggling interdiction and eradication. But despite the billions of dollars spent on these efforts, cocaine remains cheap and plentiful in the United States, indicating that perhaps the efforts are not as successful as the government hopes.

## Attacking the Source

The U.S. government's goal in its war on drugs, according to the U.S. Department of State's *International Narcotics Control Strategy Report 2007*, "is to reduce and ultimately cut off the international flow of illegal drugs" coming to the United States. It believes the most effective means of cutting off the drug supply is to start at the source—eradicating the coca fields in

Colombia. "Drugs cannot enter the system from crops that were never planted, or have been destroyed or left unharvested; without the crops there would be no need for costly enforcement and interdiction operations."[34]

> " Few crops grow in areas and under the same conditions where coca bushes thrive. "

The U.S. government, along with the government of Colombia, and to a lesser extent, the governments of Bolivia and Peru, are attempting to convince farmers to give up growing the lucrative coca bushes and plant other crops in its place. However, even with crop subsidies, the governments are not having much luck persuading the farmers to switch crops. Few crops grow in areas and under the same conditions where coca bushes thrive. But most important, farmers can sell coca leaves for far more than they can earn on any other crop, even if they receive government subsidies. According to drug policy experts at the Cato Institute, a think tank in Washington, D.C., "The cost of growing coca . . . represents such a small fraction of the final value of cocaine—less than 1 percent—that the illicit drug industry will always be able to pay farmers more than the subsidized alternatives could command."[35]

## Hand Eradication

When the U.S. and Colombian governments cannot persuade the coca farmers to give up planting and harvesting coca plants, they resort to other methods, such as sending in workers to pull out coca bushes by hand. Hand eradication is a slow, difficult, and hazardous job. Anastasia Moloney of the *New Internationalist* describes a scene in the Macarena National Park in southern Colombia, where it took 900 workers 8 months to clear coca bushes from about 7,500 acres in the park. The workers were surrounded by armed soldiers on the ground and military helicopters in the air to prevent drug traffickers from trying to stop the eradication of their coca fields. At the end of the 8 months, the 900 workers had dwindled to 200 workers; bomb attacks, land mines, and the deaths of 8 workers were not enough to keep them working, nor was the pay of $12 a day.

## Fumigation

The United States also sponsors other means of eradicating the coca crop in South America. In 2000 the Clinton administration unveiled its Plan Colombia, a 6-year plan to reduce coca cultivation by half. One of the cornerstones of the plan was aerial crop spraying—fumigating coca fields with aerial sprays of the weed killer glyphosate. U.S. State Department records show that the amount of acreage sprayed during the plan's tenure increased from 47,371 hectares in 2000 to 171,613 hectares in 2006.

But the program is highly controversial. Farmers and environmentalists assert that fumigation kills legal crops and coca bushes indiscriminately. Furthermore, glyphosate is known to contaminate the soil and has harmful effects on people who have been exposed to the spray. The U.S. State Department, however, counters that glyphosate is safe, is one of the most widely used herbicides in the world, and has been approved for general use by the Environmental Protection Agency, even when used on food crops.

Despite these intense efforts by the U.S. and Colombian governments, the amount of land under coca cultivation has not changed much over the years. The State Department's most recent estimate for land under coca cultivation (2005) is 144,000 hectares (approximately 2.5 acres equals 1 hectare). That is about the same amount of land under coca cultivation in 2002 (144,400 hectares). The acreage decreased in 2003 and 2004 (113,850 and 114,000 hectares, respectively) but then climbed back up in 2005 to where it was just a few years earlier. Government sources also estimate that production of cocaine remained fairly stable in Colombia over the last 3 to 4 years, although areas under cultivation of *Erythroxylon coca* in Bolivia increased 74 percent from 2000 to 2005.

" Fumigation kills legal crops and coca bushes indiscriminately. "

## Smuggling Interdiction

In March 2007 a Panamanian ship carrying 20 tons of cocaine and bound for Mexico was intercepted off the coast of Panama by Panamanian police, the U.S. Coast Guard, and U.S. Drug Enforcement Administration officers in a joint operation called PANEX. Valued at more than $275 million, it was the largest maritime cocaine-smuggling bust to date. A month earlier a U.S. frigate intercepted four vessels over a two-week period smuggling nearly 9 tons of cocaine in the Eastern Pacific Ocean.

In February 2007 a commercial jet took off from Caracas, Venezuela, bound for Mexico City with one ton of cocaine packed into 25 identical suitcases. Due to a tip received, the cocaine was intercepted in Mexico. Authorities believe that the drugs made it through customs checkpoints in Venezuela due to "taxes" paid by drug traffickers to security forces to allow the shipment to pass without scrutiny. The Venezuelan border with Colombia has become a "sieve,"[36] according to U.S. and South American officials, that allows Colombia cocaine to pour through without being checked. Venezuelan authorities intercepted and seized almost 5 tons of cocaine in January and February 2007.

## Cocaine Remains Plentiful

The National Drug Intelligence Center noted in its *National Drug Threat Assessment 2007* report that despite increasing record-level seizures of cocaine since 2000, cocaine remains plentiful in the United States and elsewhere. This suggests, according to the NDIC, that the countries that produce cocaine—Colombia, Peru, and Bolivia—are increasing their cocaine production at rates greater than previously believed. Furthermore, the NDIC contends that South American drug traffickers have been able to maintain their supply of cocaine and transport it with little interruption in supply or service.

> Education about drug abuse continues to be the primary tool in the war on drugs.

In addition, smuggling methods and routes into the United States have not changed due to the increased presence of U.S. and South American drug enforcement officials. According to the NDIC, the Central American and Mexican corridor is still "the predominant transit route for cocaine destined for the United States."[37] Nor have the primary modes of transporting the smuggled cocaine changed; fishing boats, and the fast and stealthy cigarette-type boats known as "go-fast" boats, are still the most common vehicles intercepted by U.S. drug enforcement agencies. However, the NDIC notes that some small changes have taken place since the turn of the twenty-first century. Cocaine smugglers are now traveling farther offshore in the Eastern Pacific Ocean, using more decoy ships and more ships that are registered in countries other than Colombia. Nevertheless, south Texas continues to be the leading point of entry for cocaine smuggled into the United States, while Atlanta is becoming a staging area for cocaine that will be distributed to dealers along the East Coast.

> " Student drug testing programs . . . can give parents and educators information about whether or not the child is using drugs. "

## Parental Involvement

On the domestic front, education about drug abuse continues to be the primary tool in the war on drugs. The President's National Drug Control Strategy maintains that no prevention program "is enough to make a decisive difference without significant parental involvement."[38] Numerous studies have found that when parents are involved with their teens, and when they keep up on the latest news about drugs and addiction, it is less likely that their child will take drugs.

Public service announcements can give parents the information they need to monitor their teens' behavior. Several community service prevention strategies allow other adults to watch over and supervise teens when their parents are not able to. By monitoring their teens' behavior, their activities, and their location—especially after school—parents can help keep their children off drugs as well as keep them safe from other risky behavior, such as sex and smoking.

Parents need to remain active and aware of student drug testing programs, which can give parents and educators information about whether or not the child is using drugs. According to the President's National Drug Control Strategy, "Screening for drug use gives young people an 'out' to say no to drugs."[39] Drug testing advocates maintain that teens will not take drugs if they know they will be tested and lose privileges, such as playing on a sports team, if they test positive for drugs. However, not everyone believes that drug tests for students are appropriate. Richard Glen Boire, codirector and legal counsel for the Center for Cognitive Liberty and Ethics, believes that forcing students to take drug tests without a suspicion of wrongdoing treats them like criminals.

## Continuing Controversy

Despite the decades-long war on drugs, several departments of the U.S. government concede that cocaine is still as readily available, as cheap, and as pure as it ever was. Yet the government still maintains a zero-tolerance policy on drug abuse. Whether the government will change its strategy of eradication, interdiction, education, and punishment remains to be seen.

# Is the War on Cocaine Effective?

> **Nothing that creates hundreds of billions of dollars of income annually and is desired by millions of people will be stopped by any nation on this earth.**

—Charles Bowden, *Down by the River: Drugs, Money, Murder, and Family.* New York: Simon and Shuster, 2002.

Charles Bowden is an author of numerous books, including two about illegal drugs. He is also a contributing editor for *Esquire* magazine and has written for several others such as *Harper's* and *Mother Jones*.

> **We are helping President [Alvaro] Uribe and the Colombian people defeat the cocaine cartels and narco-terrorists. We're providing money to help honest farmers grow legitimate crops.**

—George W. Bush, "President Bush Discusses Democracy in the Western Hemisphere," November 6, 2005. www.whitehouse.gov.

Bush is the forty-third president of the United States.

Bracketed quotes indicate conflicting positions.

* Editor's Note: While the definition of a primary source can be narrowly or broadly defined, for the purposes of Compact Research, a primary source consists of: 1) results of original research presented by an organization or researcher; 2) eyewitness accounts of events, personal experience, or work experience; 3) first-person editorials offering pundits' opinions; 4) government officials presenting political plans and/or policies; 5) representatives of organizations presenting testimony or policy.

Primary Source Quotes

**66** Large-scale eradication is an effective means of targeting trafficker networks because most growers are affected, reducing the production available to all traffickers. **99**

—Office of National Drug Control Policy, *National Drug Control Strategy Update*. Washington, DC: ONDCP, February 2005, p. 42. www.whitehousedrugpolicy.gov.

The Office of National Drug Control Policy releases an annual report detailing the administration's goals toward reducing the country's drug use with a national policy that combines enforcement, treatment, and prevention.

**66** So, are we there yet? Are we succeeding in shrinking the supply of cocaine and heroin and driving up prices? The best available evidence suggests that we are in a deep rut, spinning our wheels and going nowhere fast. **99**

—John M. Walsh, "Are We There Yet? Monitoring Progress in the U.S. War on Drugs in Latin America," *WOLA Drug War Monitor*, December 2004.

Walsh is the senior associate for the Andes and Drug Policy at the Washington Office on Latin America, a think tank in Washington, D.C., that provides information on and analysis of U.S. policies on the war on drugs, human rights, and social justice in Latin America.

**66** Our strategy in Colombia is working. We are attacking traffickers across all fronts . . . by eradication, interdiction and organizational attack. **99**

—John P. Walters, "Press Conference Announcing Guilty Pleas of Cali Cartel," September 26, 2006. www.usdoj.gov.

Walters is the director of the White House Office on National Drug Control Policy.

66 Despite the fact that the highest recorded level of co-caine interdiction and seizure was recorded in 2005— the fifth consecutive record-setting increase—there have been no sustained cocaine shortages or indications of stretched supplies in domestic drug markets. 99

—National Drug Intelligence Center, *National Drug Threat Assessment 2007*. Johnstown, PA: NDIC, October 2006. www.usdoj.gov/ndic.

Established in 1993, the National Drug Intelligence Center (NDIC) is a component of the U.S. Department of Justice and a member of the Intelligence Community. The General Counterdrug Intelligence Plan, signed by President George W. Bush in February 2000, designated NDIC as the nation's principal center for strategic domestic counterdrug intelligence.

66 Legalizing cocaine would cut off that enormous income from the terrorists' treasury. 99

—Joseph Szydlowski, "Drug Policy Needs a Fix," *Northerner,* March 29, 2006. www.thenortherner.com.

Szydlowski was a student at Northern Kentucky University at the time this essay was published.

66 Nearly a decade after large-scale spraying began in Colombia, our fumigation program is not discouraging Colombian peasants from growing coca. 99

—Adam Isacson, "The State Department's New Coca Data," March 30, 2005. www.ciponline.org.

Isacson is an expert on Colombia for the Center for International Policy in Washington, D.C.

**66With legalization, experts believe the number of cocaine addicts alone could jump beyond the number of alcoholics.99**

—Joseph A. Califano Jr., "Q: Should Illegal Drugs Be Criminalized? No," *PBS: Moyers on Addiction, Close to Home.* www.wnet.org.

Califano is the president of the National Center on Addiction and Substance Abuse at Columbia University (CASA). He has served as U.S. secretary of health, education, and welfare.

**66Drug testing is ineffective, undermines trust between adults and youth, and may discourage kids from taking part in extracurricular activities and sports.99**

—Bob Curley, "Student Drug Testing: Compassion or Punishment?" February 6, 2004. www.jointogether.org.

Curley is the news editor for Join Together Online, a program of the Boston University School of Public Health that works to advance effective alcohol and drug policy, prevention, and treatment.

**66Testing students who participate in extracurricular activities is a reasonably effective means of addressing the School District's legitimate concerns in preventing, deterring, and detecting drug use.99**

—Clarence J. Thomas et al., *Board of Education of Independent School District No. 92 of Pottawatomie County et al. v. Earls et al.*, June 27, 2002.

Thomas is a justice on the U.S. Supreme Court.

66 Most, if not all, of the violence from the drug trade stems from people trying to facilitate the business of drugs. . . . If drugs like coke and crack were legal, this facilitation crime stops almost instantly. 99

—Wilton D. Alston, "Why Is There a War on Drugs?" October 5, 2006. http://lewrockwell.com.

Alston is a syndicated columnist who studies libertarian philosophy and is a research scientist in transportation safety.

66 Parents and other caregivers need to do more than simply talk about drugs and alcohol. They also need to act—by monitoring the behavior of teen children, knowing where their teenagers are at all times, particularly after school, and knowing whom they are with and what they are doing. Such techniques have proved remarkably effective in keeping teenagers away from drugs. 99

—Office of National Drug Control Policy, *National Drug Control Strategy Update 2005*. Washington, DC: ONDCP, February 2005.

The principal purpose of the Office of National Drug Control Policy is to establish policies, priorities, and objectives for the nation's drug control program. The goals of the program are to reduce illicit drug use, manufacturing, and trafficking, drug-related crime and violence, and drug-related health consequences.

# Facts and Illustrations

## Is the War on Cocaine Effective?

- Colombian traffickers provide up to **90 percent** of the cocaine used in the United States and other world markets.

- Due to its **1,300-mile porous border** with Colombia, cocaine is increasingly being smuggled through Venezuela on its way to global markets.

- U.S. officials estimate that over **90 percent** of the cocaine departing South America for the United States passes through Mexico.

- Demand for cocaine in Europe reached **all-time highs** by late 2006/ early 2007. Western Africa has become a transfer point for cocaine smuggled out of South America on its way to Europe.

- Since 2000, the United States has spent nearly **$3 billion** on programs to fight drug trafficking and to train the Colombian military to battle insurgents who control much of the drug trade.

- While coca production in Bolivia and Peru fell by more than 50 percent from 1987 to 1999, production in Colombia increased over **1,140 percent**.

# Retail Cocaine Prices in the United States Declining

Demand for cocaine in the United States has been stable, if not actually rising. The number of cocaine users in the United States is increasing, and the age of first use is declining. However, cocaine supplies continue to be readily available in the United States. The result is that wholesale and retail prices for cocaine were at or near their all-time lows.

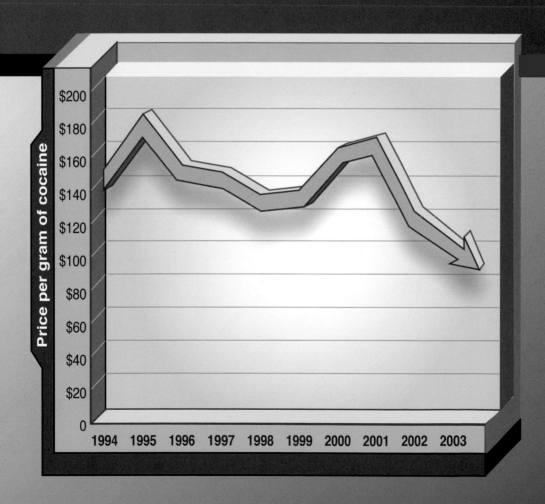

Source: Latin America Working Group Education Fund, Center for International Policy, Washington Office on Latin America, and U.S. Office on Colombia, *Blueprint for a New Colombia Policy*, 2005.

- While cocaine has been responsible for the harm caused to both producers and users of the drug, the coca leaf—which produces cocaine—has been a real boon to many **rural farmers** in South America who earn more growing coca than they can from any other legitimate crop.

## How Cocaine Gets to the United States

Data from drug seizures indicate that despite record-level cocaine busts, drug traffickers are not changing their smuggling routes. Most cocaine seizures in 2005 occurred in the Eastern Pacific and Western Caribbean, usually while the shipment was en route to Mexico. Nearly 90 percent of all cocaine smuggled out of Colombia enters the United States via the Central America–Mexico corridor. South Texas is the number one point of entry for cocaine into the United States.

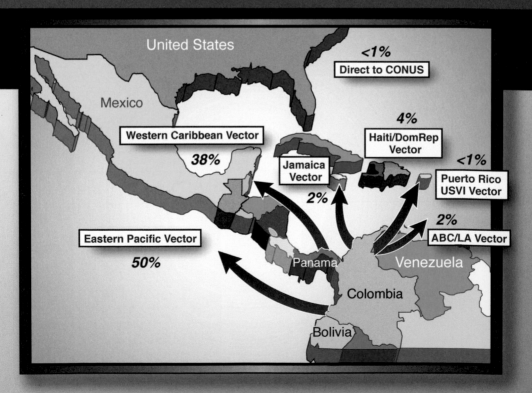

Source: *Interagency Assessment of Cocaine Movement*, Midyear CY 2006 Update.

## Coca Eradication

The Office of National Drug Control Policy uses satellite imaging to survey coca cultivation in Colombia. In 2005, it expanded the area it surveyed by 81 percent. While it found that coca cultivation had declined by 8 percent in the area it had surveyed in 2004, it found an additional 39,000 acres of coca under cultivation in the expanded survey area, which could potentially yield 545 metric tons of pure cocaine.

| Year | Hectares under cultivation | Percent Decrease |
|------|----------------------------|------------------|
| 1998 | 101,800 | 28% |
| 1999 | 122,500 | 20% |
| 2000 | 136,200 | 11% |
| 2001 | 169,800 | 25% |
| 2002 | 144,450 | (−15%) |
| 2003 | 113,850 | (−21%) |
| 2004 | 114,100 | 0.2% |

Source: Office of National Drug Control Policy, 2005. www.whitehousedrugpolicy.gov.

- New "**dipstick**" drug tests can detect cocaine and other illicit drugs in saliva, urine, or blood.

- More than half of the student athletes at a high school in California said in a 2006 survey that the school's random drug testing made it easier for them to say "no" to drugs. More than **80 percent** said they would have used drugs or alcohol if their school did not have a random drug testing program.

# Student Drug-Testing Sites

Many schools across the country have instituted student testing as a way to maintain drug-free schools and ensure that students who use drugs get the help they need. In his 2004 State of the Union Address, President Bush announced a new program that will provide grants to schools that apply for help in running drug-testing programs. This map shows where the grants for drug testing have been implemented.

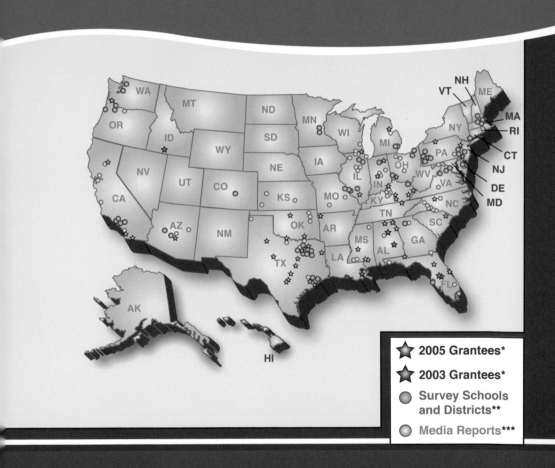

★ 2005 Grantees*

★ 2003 Grantees*

● Survey Schools and Districts**

● Media Reports***

* Department of Education grantees.

** School districts and private schools that identified themselves as conducting student drug testing in a 2003 survey conducted by the Office of National Drug Control Policy.

*** Schools that were identified in media reports as conducting student drug testing.

Source: Office of National Drug Control Policy, 2005. www.whitehousedrugpolicy.gov

# Key People and Advocacy Groups

**Cali Cartel:** The Cali Cartel is an organization of cocaine drug lords based in Cali, Colombia. The Cali Cartel was organized in the 1970s by Gilberto Rodríguez Orejuela and his brother, Miguel Rodríguez Orejuela. The Cali Cartel was a bitter rival of the Medellín Cartel. After the death of Pablo Escobar, the Medellín Cartel's drug lord, the Cali Cartel took over and controlled nearly all the cocaine production and trafficking in Colombia.

**Drug Free America Foundation:** The Drug Free America Foundation is a drug prevention and policy organization committed to developing policies and laws that will reduce illegal drug use, drug addiction, and drug-related injuries and deaths. It believes that drug legalization will be harmful to the United States.

**Pablo Escobar:** Escobar was the Colombian cocaine kingpin and leader of the Medellín Cartel in Colombia. He is said to have been one of the most brutal and ruthless drug lords, responsible for ordering the murders of dozens of judges, politicians, and rivals. *Forbes* magazine listed him as the seventh richest man in the world in 1989 with a daily income of $6.4 million. He was killed in 1993 during a shoot-out with a Colombia police task force in Medellín.

**Sigmund Freud:** An early proponent of cocaine, Freud declared it "a miracle drug."

**James Inciardi:** Inciardi is the director of the Center for Drug and Alcohol Studies at the University of Delaware and a member of the Internal Policy Committee, Executive Office of the President, Office of the National Drug Control Policy. He has written numerous books in the areas of substance abuse, criminology, and public policy.

**Karl Koller:** Koller was an ophthalmology intern who, in 1884, discovered that cocaine was an ideal anesthetic for eye surgery.

**Alan I. Leshner:** Leshner is the former director of the National Institute on Drug Abuse, a federal agency that works to prevent drug abuse and addition.

**Medellín Cartel:** The Medellín Cartel is an organized network of Colombia cocaine traffickers, run by Pablo Escobar, and said to have controlled 80 percent of the world's cocaine production. It was at the peak of its power during the 1970s and 1980s, at which time the cartel was estimated to bring in $60 million a month from cocaine.

**William Cope Moyers:** Moyers, the son of journalist Bill Moyers, was himself a journalist who became addicted to cocaine. He went through recovery at the Hazelden Foundation, a rehabilitation center for alcoholics and drug addicts in Minnesota, and eventually became the vice president of external affairs at Hazelden.

**Ethan Nadelmann:** Nadelmann is a proponent of drug policy reform both in the United States and abroad. He is the founder and executive director of the Drug Policy Alliance, an organization promoting drug reform policy and alternatives to the war on drugs.

**National Drug Court Institute:** The National Drug Court Institute is an organization that provides training for drug court professions, supports research for more effective drug court policies and procedures, and disseminates research, evaluations, and commentary on drug courts.

**National Drug Intelligence Center:** Established in 1993, the National Drug Intelligence Center (NDIC) is a component of the U.S. Department of Justice and a member of the Intelligence Community. The General Counterdrug Intelligence Plan, signed by President George W. Bush in February 2000, designated NDIC as the nation's principal center for strategic domestic counterdrug intelligence.

**National Institute on Drug Abuse (NIDA):** NIDA is part of the U.S. Department of Health and Human Services, and works to prevent drug abuse and addiction in the United States. The organization supports research studies on abuse and addiction and works to educate the public about the results of this research.

**Jorge, Fabio, and Juan David Ochoa:** These three brothers were cocaine traffickers with the Medellín Cartel in Colombia during the late 1970s. All three served time in jail in Colombia and after their release in 1997, retired to their horse and cattle ranches. Fabio was rearrested by Colombia police in 1999 and extradited to the United States in 2001. He was convicted of drug conspiracy and money laundering charges in 2003 and sentenced to 365 months in prison.

**Office of National Drug Control Policy:** The principal purpose of the Office of National Drug Control Policy is to establish policies, priorities, and objectives for the nation's drug control program. The goals of the program are to reduce illicit drug use, manufacturing, and trafficking; drug-related crime and violence; and drug-related health consequences.

**Gilberto and Miguel Rodríguez Orejuela:** Gilberto Orejuela was the founder and leader of the Cali Cartel, a network of cocaine traffickers in Colombia. He and his brother Miguel Rodríguez Orejuela were captured by Colombian police in Cali in 1995 and sentenced to 15 years in prison, later reduced to 7 years. After their release in 2002 they were rearrested in 2003 and extradited to the United States. In September 2006 the brothers were sentenced to 30 years in prison for their cocaine trafficking.

**Karen P. Tandy:** Tandy is administrator of the Drug Enforcement Administration. She has pledged to help carry out the administration's war on drugs.

**John P. Walters:** Walters was sworn in as the director of the White House Office of National Drug Control Policy in 2001. As the nation's "drug czar," Walters coordinates all aspects of federal drug programs and spending. Since taking office Walters has aggressively pursued the goal of reducing teen and adult cocaine use.

**White House Office of National Drug Control Policy (ONDCP):** The ONDCP was established in 1988. Its goal is to eradicate illicit drug manufacture, sale, and use in the United States. It also works to eliminate drug-related crime, violence, and health consequences.

# Chronology

**1504**
Amerigo Vespucci publishes the first account of Indians on the island of Santa Margarita chewing coca leaves.

**1548**
The Spanish conquistadors use the Incas to mine silver in Potosi, Bolivia, and pay them with over 1 million kilograms of coca leaves.

**1859**
Albert Niemann develops an improved process to purify coca leaves into cocaine. He names the alkaloid cocaine.

**1884**
Sigmund Freud writes *Über Coca* in which he describes the beneficial effects of cocaine.

**1904**
The Coca-Cola company stops using fresh coca leaves in its recipe for the drink and uses "spent" leaves that were left over from the cocaine extraction process.

**1961**
The United Nations passes the Single Convention on Narcotic Drugs, an international treaty that prohibits the manufacture and distribution of illegal drugs such as cocaine. The treaty will go into effect in 1964.

**1970**
Congress passes the Controlled Substances Act, which regulates the manufacture, importation, possession, and distribution of cocaine and other drugs in the United States.

**1970s**
The Cali and Medellín Cartels—a network of drug-trafficking organizations—are established in Colombia to meet the demand for cocaine.

**1500**   **1650**   **1800**   **1950**   **1970**   **1975**

**1609**
Because the Incas refuse to work in the silver mine without being paid in coca leaves, the Catholic Church imposes a 10 percent tax on the sale of the leaves to the Indians.

**1567**
At the Second Council of Lima, the Church tries again to ban coca production, calling coca "a plant that the Devil invented for the total destruction of the natives."

**1552**
At the First Council of Lima the Catholic Church attempts to ban the use of coca leaves, claiming it is "the work of the devil."

**1886**
Coca-Cola, containing cocaine, is invented by John Stith Pemberton as an nonalcoholic alternative to Vin Mariani.

**1914**
The Harrison Narcotics Act is passed by Congress and bans the use of cocaine without a prescription by a doctor.

**1969**
In the movie *Easy Rider*, actors Dennis Hopper and Peter Fonda sell cocaine to music producer Phil Spector, the first time cocaine is shown in modern movies.

**1971**
President Richard M. Nixon declares a war on drugs. For the only time in history, more money is spent on drug treatment than on law enforcement.

**1975**
Colombian police seize the largest shipment of cocaine to date—600 kilograms—at an airport in Cali. In response, 40 people are massacred in Medellín.

**1979**
The United States and Colombia sign a treaty that makes drug smuggling an extraditable offense. The treaty is ratified by the U.S. Senate in 1981.

**1980**
Comedian Richard Pryor sets himself on fire while freebasing cocaine, bringing the technique of converting cocaine to freebase to the attention of the mainstream world.

**1988**
Panamanian general Manuel Noriega is indicted in the United States for money laundering and drug smuggling for allowing cocaine shipments through Panama.

**1983**
The largest shipment ever—3,906 pounds—of cocaine is seized from an airport hangar in Miami.

**1991**
New Colombian constitution bans extraditing drug smugglers to the United States. Pablo Escobar, leader of the Medellín Cartel, surrenders to Colombian police.

**2000**
President Bill Clinton announces the delivery of $1.3 billion in aid to Colombia to help fight the cocaine industry and drug traffickers.

**1985**
Crack makes its first appearance. Its popularity soars. An article in the medical journal *New England Journal of Medicine* discusses the effects of prenatal crack use on infants. The media coins the term *crack baby*.

**1995**
The U.S. Sentencing Commission recommends equalizing the mandatory minimum sentences for crack and cocaine. Five of the top leaders of the Cali Cartel are arrested.

**1980**     **1985**     **1990**     **1995**     **2000**     **2005**

**1993**
Pablo Escobar, the Medellín Cartel's top drug lord, is killed during a shoot-out with Colombian police. The Cali Cartel becomes the most powerful drug-trafficking organization in Colombia.

**1984**
The Drug Enforcement Administraton and the Colombian police find and destroy a cocaine laboratory operated by the Medellín Cartel deep in the Colombia jungle. Almost 14 tons of cocaine and seven airplanes, worth $1.2 billion, are destroyed in the bust.

**2007**
Cocaine continues to be the second most popular illicit drug—behind marijuana.

**1989**
President George H.W. Bush creates the Office of National Drug Control Policy and names William Bennett as the nation's first "drug czar."

**1982**
Medellín Cartel drug lord Pablo Escobar makes a deal with Panamanian general Manuel Noriega that allows Escobar to ship cocaine through Panama for $100,000 per load.

**1986**
Believing that crack is a more addictive and dangerous drug than cocaine, Congress passes the Anti-Drug Abuse Act, which sets mandatory minimum sentences for crack and cocaine possession.

**1998**
Bolivia begins implementation of Plan Dignidad, a $1.3 billion program sponsored by the United States to eradicate the coca bush in the country.

# Related Organizations

### American Civil Liberties Union (ACLU)

125 Broad St., 18th Floor

New York, NY 10004-2400

phone: (212) 549-2500 • Web site: www.aclu.org

The ACLU is a national organization that works to defend Americans' civil rights guaranteed by the U.S. Constitution. It provides legal defense, research, and education. The ACLU's goal is to end punitive drug policies that cause the widespread violation of constitutional and human rights, as well as unprecedented levels of incarceration. Its publications include the report *Cracks in the System: 20 Years of the Unjust Federal Crack Cocaine Law.*

### American Council for Drug Education (ACDE)

164 W. 74th St.

New York, NY 10023

phone: (800) 488-DRUG (3784) • (212) 595-5810, ext. 7860

fax: (212) 595-2553 • Web site: www.acde.org

The American Council for Drug Education informs the public about the harmful effects of abusing drugs and alcohol. It gives the public access to scientifically based, compelling prevention programs and materials. ACDE has resources for parents, youth, educators, prevention professionals, employers, health care professionals, and other concerned community members who are working to help America's youth avoid the dangers of drug and alcohol abuse.

### Cocaine Anonymous

PO Box 492000

Los Angeles, CA 90049-8000

phone: (310) 559-5833

fax: (310) 449-2554

e-mail cawso@ca.org • Web site: www.ca.org

Cocaine Anonymous is a 12-step program for cocaine addicts who want to stop using the drug. It holds group meetings, similar to those of Alcoholics Anonymous, in which addicts can share their experiences, strengths, and hopes in a supportive environment. Among its publications are the pamphlets *Tips for Staying Clean & Sober* and *Crack.*

## Drug Enforcement Administration (DEA)

700 Army Navy Dr.

Arlington, VA 22202

phone: (202) 307-1000

Web site: www.usdoj.gov/dea

The DEA is the federal agency charged with enforcing the nation's drug laws. The agency concentrates on stopping the smuggling and distribution of narcotics in the United States and abroad. It publishes the *Drug Enforcement Magazine* three times a year.

## Drug Policy Alliance

70 W. 36th St., 16th Floor

New York, NY 10018

phone: (212) 613-8020 • fax: (212) 613-8021

Web site: www.lindesmith.org

The Drug Policy Alliance believes the war on drugs is doing more harm than good. The organization's goals are to change public attitudes and promote legislative drug policy reforms on the state level. Among its many publications are *Safety First: A Reality-Based Approach to Teens and Drugs, Repeating Mistakes of the Past: Another Mycoherbicide Research Bill,* and *Making Sense of Student Drug Testing.*

## DrugSense/Media Awareness Project (MAP)

PO Box 651

Porterville, CA 93258

phone: (800) 266-5759

e-mail: info@drugsense.org • Web site: www.drugsense.org

DrugSense/MAP is an international network of activists dedicated to drug policy reform, with an emphasis on impacting public opinion and media coverage of drug policy issues. It opposes the criminal justice/prosecution/interdiction model of drug policy and favors a more liberal approach. MAP publishes the weekly *DrugSense* newsletter and makes tens of thousands of drug policy-related articles available on its Web site.

## National Center on Addiction and Substance Abuse (CASA)

Columbia University, 152 W. 57th St.

New York, NY 10019-3310

phone: (212) 841-5200 • fax: (212) 956-8020

Web site: www.casacolumbia.org

CASA is a private nonprofit organization that works to educate the public about the hazards of drug abuse. The organization supports treatment as the best way to reduce chemical dependency. Its publications include the book *High Society: How Substance Abuse Ravages America and What to Do About It*, the report *Wasting the Best and the Brightest: Substance Abuse at America's Colleges and Universities*, and the newsletter *CASA Inside*.

## National Institute on Drug Abuse (NIDA)

U.S. Department of Health and Human Services

5600 Fishers Ln.

Rockville, MD 20857

phone: (301) 443-6245 • e-mail: Information@nida.nih.gov

Web site: www.nida.nih.gov

NIDA supports and conducts research on drug abuse—including the yearly *Monitoring the Future Survey*—to improve addiction prevention, treatment, and policy efforts. It publishes the bimonthly *NIDA Notes* newsletter, the periodic *NIDA Capsules* fact sheets, and a catalog of research reports and public education materials, such as the fact sheet "Crack and Cocaine," and the research report *Cocaine: Abuse and Addiction*.

## Office of National Drug Control Policy

Drugs and Crime Clearinghouse, PO Box 6000

Rockville, MD 20849-6000

phone: (800) 666-3332 • fax: (301) 519-5212

Web site: www.whitehousedrugpolicy.gov

The Office of National Drug Control Policy is responsible for formulating the government's national drug strategy and the president's antidrug policy as well as coordinating the federal agencies responsible for stopping drug trafficking. *The President's National Drug Control Strategy* is available on the Web site.

## Partnership for a Drug-Free America

405 Lexington Ave., Suite 1601

New York, NY 10174

phone: (212) 922-1560 • fax: (212) 922-1570

Web site: www.drugfreeamerica.org

The Partnership for a Drug-Free America is a nonprofit organization that utilizes media communication to reduce demand for illicit drugs in America. Best known for its national antidrug advertising campaign, the partnership works to "unsell" drugs to children and to prevent drug use among kids. Its Web site publishes information guides about drugs as well as personal narratives about drug use.

## RAND Drug Policy Research Center

1776 Main St., PO Box 2138

Santa Monica, CA 90407-2138

e-mail: dprc@rand.org • Web site: www.rand.org

The DPRC conducts research to help community leaders and public officials develop more effective ways of dealing with drug problems. It publishes the electronic monthly newsletter *DPRC Insights* that highlights the specific findings made by RAND researchers in the field of drug policy. Its publications include the reports *Prenatal Cocaine Exposure: Scientific Considerations and Policy Implications; Cocaine, Marijuana, and Heroin*; and *College Students' Use of Cocaine.*

# For Further Research

## Books

Nate Blakeslee, *Tulia: Race, Cocaine, and Corruption in a Small Texas Town.* New York: Public Affairs, 2005.

Belen Boville and Lorena Terando, *The Cocaine War in Context: Drugs and Politics.* New York: Agora, 2004.

Patrick Clawson and Renssaelaer W. Lee, *The Andean Cocaine Industry.* New York: Palgrave Macmillan, 2006.

Gary L. Fisher, *Rethinking Our War on Drugs: Candid Talk About Controversial Issues.* Westport, CT: Praeger, 2006.

Jeff Henderson, *Cooked: From the Streets to the Stove, from Cocaine to Foie Gras.* New York: William Morrow, 2007.

Stephen Hyde and Geno Zanetti, eds., *White Lines: Writers on Cocaine.* New York: Thunder's Mouth, 2002.

James Inciardi, *The War on Drugs III: The Continuing Saga of the Mysteries and Miseries of Intoxication, Addiction, Crime, and Public Policy.* Boston, MA: Allyn and Bacon, 2002.

Steven B. Karch, *A Brief History of Cocaine*, 2nd ed. Boca Raton, FL: CRC, 2005.

Robin Kirk, *More Terrible than Death: Massacres, Drugs, and America's War in Colombia.* New York: Public Affairs, 2003.

Sandra Augustyn Lawton, ed., *Drug Information for Teens: Health Tips About the Physical and Mental Effects of Substance Abuse.* Detroit, MI: Omnigraphics, 2006.

Charles F. Levinthal, *Drugs, Behavior, and Modern Society.* Boston, MA: Allyn and Bacon, 2005.

Tim Madge, *White Mischief: A Cultural History of Cocaine.* New York: Thunder's Mouth, 2004.

William Cope Moyers, *Broken: My Story of Addiction and Redemption.* New York: Viking, 2006.

Ronald K. Siegel, *Intoxication: The Universal Drive for Mind-Altering Substances.* Rochester, VT: Park Street, 2005.

Dominic Streatfeild, *Cocaine: An Unauthorized Biography*. New York: Picador, 2003.

Jerry Tervalon and Gary Phillips, eds., *The Cocaine Chronicles*. New York: Akashic Books, 2005.

Janet Y. Thomas, *Educating Drug-Exposed Children: The Aftermath of the Crack-Baby Crisis*. London: Routledge, 2004.

Stan Zimmerman, *A History of Smuggling in Florida: Rum Runners and Cocaine Cowboys*. Charleston, SC: History Press, 2006.

## Periodicals

Sudie E. Back, Regana Contini, and Kathleen T. Brady, "Substance Abuse in Women: Does Gender Matter?" *Psychiatric Times*, January 2007.

Cate Baily, "Cocaine: Big White Lies," *Junior Scholastic*, October 27, 2003.

Mariah Blake, "The Damage Done: Crack Babies Talk Back," *Columbia Journalism Review*, September/October 2004.

Joel Brinkley, "Anti-Drug Gains in Colombia Don't Reduce Flow to U.S.," *New York Times*, April 28, 2005.

Peter Canby, "Latin America's Longest War," *Nation*, August 16, 2004.

Lynette Clemetson, "Congress Is Expected to Revisit Sentencing Laws," *New York Times*, January 9, 2007.

*Congressional Digest*, "Colombian Drug Threat," January 2003.

Joshua Davis, "The Mystery of the Coca Plant That Wouldn't Die," *Wired*, November 2004, www.wired.com.

Stephen J. Dubner and Steven D. Levitt, "Up in Smoke," *New York Times*, August 7, 2005.

Steven Dudley, "On the Road with the FARC," *Progressive*, November 2003.

*Economist*, "The Price of Powder," November 11, 2004.

Gary Fields, "Sentencing Guidelines Face New Scrutiny," *Wall Street Journal*, December 26, 2006.

Dana Harman, "The War on Drugs: Ambushed in Jamundí," *Christian Science Monitor*, September 27, 2006.

*Harper's Magazine*, "Blow, Winds, and Crack Your Checks," May 2004.

Chris Kraul and Sebastian Rotella, "Venezuela's Rising Role in Drug Transit Worries U.S.," *Los Angeles Times*, March 21, 2007.

Stephen Leahy, "Rivers of Coke," *Wired*, August 5, 2005. www.wired.com.

Steven D. Levitt and Kevin M. Murphy, "How Bad Was Crack Cocaine? The Economics of an Illicit Drug Market," *Capital Ideas*, April 2006. www.chicagogsb.edu.

David C. Lewis, "Stop Perpetuating the 'Crack Baby' Myth," *Brown University Digest of Addiction Theory and Application*, August 2004.

*New Scientist*, "While There's a Market," September 9, 2006.

Lynn Paltrow, "Battle Wombs: Why Some Drug Babies Are More Equal than Others," *RAND Review*, Fall 2002.

Kristen Philipkoski, "Designing Drugs to Swat Addiction," *Wired*, March 29, 2004. www.wired.com.

Craig Reinarman and Harry G. Levine, "Crack in the Rearview Mirror: Deconstructing Drug War Mythology," *Social Justice*, vol. 31, nos. 1–2, 2004.

Sebastian Rotella and Chris Kraul, "A Drug's Worrisome Detour," *Los Angeles Times*, March 14, 2007.

Eric E. Sterling, "Take Another Crack at the Cocaine Law," *Los Angeles Times*, November 13, 2006.

Maia Szalavitz, "The Demon Seed That Wasn't: Debunking the 'Crack Baby' Myth," *City Limits*, March 2004.

Carlos Villalon, "Cocaine Country," *National Geographic*, July 2004.

Kate Wheeler, "Coca Fiend," *Outside*, October 2004.

## Internet Sources

*Cocaine.org*, "In Search of the Big Bang." www.cocaine.org.

National Institute on Drug Abuse, "InfoFacts: Crack and Cocaine," May 2006. www.drugabuse.gov.

Office of National Drug Control Policy, "Drug Facts: Cocaine," 2006. www.whitehousedrugpolicy.gov.

Judith Schaffer, "Cocaine Use During Pregnancy: Its Effects on Infant Development and Implications for Adoptive Parents," August 4, 2004. www.nysccc.org.

U.S. Sentencing Commission, *Sourcebook of Federal Sentencing Statistics 2006*. www.ussc.gov.

Deborah J. Vagins and Jesselyn McCurdy, "Cracks in the System: Twenty Years of the Unjust Federal Crack Cocaine Law," 2006. www.aclu.org.

# Source Notes

## Overview

1. eMedicineHealth, *Cocaine Abuse Overview*, August 10, 2005. www.emedicine health.com.
2. Quoted in Tupay Katari, "Coca: An Andean Tradition," testimony before the United Nations Commission on Human Rights, Sub-Commission on Prevention of Discrimination and Protection of Minorities Working Group on Indigenous Populations, July 1993. http://leda.lycaeum.org.
3. Quoted in Ernest Jones, *The Life and Work of Sigmund Freud: Volume I (1856–1900)*. New York: BasicBooks, 1953, p. 81.
4. Quoted in Ann Holmes, *Psychological Effects of Cocaine and Crack Addiction*. Philadelphia: Chelsea House, 1999, p. 9.
5. *New York Medical Journal*, "Mental Sequelae of the Harrison Law," 102, May 15, 1915, p. 1,014.
6. John P. Morgan and Lynn Zimmer, "The Social Pharmacology of Smokeable Cocaine: Not All It's Cracked Up to Be" in Craig Reinarman and Harry G. Levine, eds., *Crack in America: Demon Drugs and Social Justice*. Berkeley: University of California Press, 1997, p. 134. www.druglibrary.org.
7. *USA Today*, June 16, 1986, quoted in James A. Inciardi, *The War on Drugs III: The Continuing Saga of the Mysteries and Miseries of Intoxication, Addiction, Crime, and Public Policy*. Boston: Allyn and Bacon, 2002, p. 151.
8. Quoted in Mariah Blake, "The Damage Done: Crack Babies Talk Back,"

*Columbia Journalism Review*, September/October 2004.
9. Charles Krauthammer, "Children of Cocaine," *Washington Post*, July 30, 1989, p. C7.
10. NIDA, "Cocaine Abuse and Addiction." National Institute on Drug Abuse, "Cocaine Abuse and Addiction," *Research Report Series*, Rev. November 2004. www. nida.nih.gov.
11. NIDA, "Cocaine Abuse and Addiction."
12. Gary E. Johnson, "Stop Arresting People for Bad Choices," *Cato Policy Report*, vol. 21, no. 6, November/December 1999. www.cato.org.
13. John P. Walters, "Don't Legalize Drugs," *Wall Street Journal*, July 19, 2002.

## Is Cocaine and Crack Addiction a Serious Problem?

14. Quoted in Jones, *The Life and Work of Sigmund Freud*, p. 84.
15. Fast-Times, "Cocaine: What Is It?" www.fast-times.co.nz.
16. Robert L. Dupont, *The Selfish Brain: Learning from Addiction*. Center City, MN: Hazelden, 2000, p. 159.
17. Quoted in Lori Whitten, "Cocaine Craving Activates Brain Reward Structures; Cocaine 'High' Dampens Them," *NIDA Notes*, vol. 21, no. 2, February 2007, p 2.
18. "Cocaine: What Is It?" www.fast-times. co.nz.
19. Karen P. Tandy, "Marijuana: The Myths Are Killing Us," *Police Chief*, March 2005.
20. Andrew R. Morral, Daniel F. McCaffrey, and Susan M. Paddock, "Reassessing the Marijuana Gateway Effect,"

*Addiction*, vol. 97, no. 12, December 2002, pp. 1,509–11.

21. Quoted in *Alcoholism & Drug Abuse Weekly*, "Cocaine Use Could Raise Risk of Parkinson's," January 2, 2006.

## Are Punishments for Cocaine and Crack Administered Fairly?

22. Stephen J. Dubner and Steven D. Levitt, "Up in Smoke," *New York Times*, August 7, 2005.
23. U.S. House Judiciary Subcommittee on Crime, Report 99-845, Part 1, September 19, 1986, pp. 11–12.
24. Quoted in U.S. Sentencing Commission, *Report to the Congress: Cocaine and Federal Sentencing Policy*, May 2002, p. 8.
25. Larry D. Thompson, testimony before the U.S. Sentencing Commission, March 19, 2002.
26. Dubner and Levitt, "Up in Smoke."
27. Krauthammer, "Children of Cocaine."
28. Paul Stevens, *Crystal M. Ferguson v. City of Charleston*, 532 US 67, March 21, 2001.

## How Should Cocaine and Crack Addiction Be Treated?

29. Quoted in Beverly Conyers, "The Stranger You Love," *eNotAlone*, 2003. www.enotalone.com.
30. Conyers, "The Stranger You Love."
31. Quoted in Robert Mathias, "Alcohol-Treatment Medication May Help Reduce Cocaine Abuse Among Heroin Treatment Patients," *NIDA Notes*, vol. 16, no. 1, March 2001.
32. International Society of Interpersonal Psychotherapy, "IPT for Patients Who Abuse Drugs." www.interpersonalpsychotherapy.org.
33. C.P. O'Brien and A.T. McLellan, "Myths About the Treatment of Addiction," *Lancet*, vol. 347, 1996.

## Is the War on Cocaine Effective?

34. Bureau of International Narcotics and Law Enforcement Affairs, *International Narcotics Control Strategy Report 2007*, March 2007. www.state.gov.
35. Ted Galen Carpenter and Ian Vásquez, *Cato Handbook on Policy*, 6th ed. Washington, DC: Cato Institute, 2005, p. 602.
36. Chris Kraul and Sebastian Rotella, "Venezuela's Rising Role in Drug Transit Worries U.S.," *Los Angeles Times*, March 21, 2007.
37. Kraul and Rotella, "Venezuela's Rising Role in Drug Transit."
38. Office of National Drug Control Policy, *President's National Drug Control Strategy*, Washington, DC: The White House, February 2005. www.whitehousedrugpolicy.gov.
39. Office of National Drug Control Policy, *President's National Drug Control Strategy*, Washington, DC: The White House, February 2006. www.whitehousedrugpolicy.gov.

# List of Illustrations

# Index

# About the Author

Tamara L. Roleff is a freelance writer living in Southern California. She has written numerous research books on drugs and related subjects.